Recall Elections:

From Alexander Hamilton to Gavin Newsom

By Joshua Spivak

FOR AMELIA:

MAY YOU STAY FOREVER IN THE FOG

LOST IN SPACE-TIME

Contents

Introduction

Should schools stay open or closed during a pandemic? Should the government take a more adversarial role with labor unions? Is there any way to stop the KKK from taking over a government? What happens with a Senator who flips his vote on a stadium tax? Should a village leader be allowed to appoint his girlfriend to the council? And should a school board member charged with attempted murder and pimping still serve in office?

Some of these questions may be earth-shaking to the populace. Others may seem like one of a million arguments that occur on the local level every year. But these specific problems were incendiary enough to lead voters to spend their time and money collecting signatures to get a new vote on the ballot in order to kick out the offending official.

California's nearly 40 million people will soon decide whether to remove Governor Gavin Newsom, the second recall election of a governor in 18 years. This recall has the potential to flip the nation's biggest state and the world's fifth largest economy from Democratic control to Republican, with many possible significant policy changes. And while California has become the ultimate Democratic state, as we'll see, the recall's most powerful point in its favor is how often it works.

The previous recall in 2003 of Gray Davis, with his replacement by movie star Arnold Schwarzenegger, was arguably the biggest political story of the year and felt like a brand new event. For most people it was, as the recall elections seemed odd and new. But the reality is they have been around as an idea since Roman times and have been in America almost since the first colonists founded the Massachusetts Bay Colony.

At times, the recall has become a prominent subject of fierce political debate – it played a major role in the 1912 Presidential Election. But for most of its existence it has either been defunct, dormant or buried so that people may have forgotten it existed. In recent decades it has seen a revival and become a prominent player, if still a side-show, in American politics. Increasingly on the state-level, political parties have looked at the recall as a shortcut to get back into power, though frequently to their own regret. But the reasons for its resurgence are unclear.

While partisanship is cited, technology and the ability to quickly organize people may be a prime motivation for the recall revival. This jump in recalls may be a global phenomenon. The presidents of Venezuela and Romania survived recall votes, Peru has witnessed a boom in recalls,[1] and just in the past year, we have seen the ousters of MPs in the UK and mayors in Taiwan through recall elections.

In nearly every instance, the recall's use engenders controversy. The ability to cut short an

---

[1] Yanina Welp and Laurence Whitehead, "The Recall Revival and Its Mixed implications for Democracy: Evidence from Latin America," in The Politics of Recall Elections, ed. Yanina Welp and Laurence Whitehead, Palgrave MacMillian, 2020. P. 159.

elected official's term is a powerful one, but there is no grand philosophical reason that it should be so controversial of an idea. It's not like Moses came down from Sinai decreeing that a city council member must be able to receive four full years in office – no more, no less – before facing the voters again. In many parliamentary systems, the party in power can call a snap election to go to the voters early. In the US, there have been repeated changes in the lengths of terms of office for different officials. The recall was adopted in some places specifically to also sell an extension in term length.

After centuries of discussion, the recall is still a subject of fierce debate, one that involves an enormous amount of ideological flip-flopping. Plenty of people decried the 2003 California Governor Gray Davis recall as a misuse of the device and cheered the 2012 Wisconsin Governor Scott Walker one as just – or vice versa for Republicans.

Voters themselves accept this dissonance. In one Wisconsin exit poll, 60% thought the recall should be reserved only for crimes and malfeasance. Another 10% of voters thought there should be no recall at all. Despite these presumably 70% of voters, Walker only got 53% of the vote. We saw similar numbers in a recent poll in California, where 69% of voters believe the recall is a waste of money, and 60% feel that recalls should be limited to cases of crimes and malfeasance.[2]

Plenty of voters either felt Walker (and likely Newsom) committed crimes worthy of being removed or instead decided that their own desire for limitations on the recall shouldn't stop them from voting their own way.

Modes of Representation: Is it true that: "The Wise Man is Preferable to the Prophet"[3]?

"We did not send him there to vote his conscience, we did not send him there to do the right thing, whatever he said he was doing. We sent him there to represent us, and we feel very strongly that he did not represent us." — Dave Ball, Washington County Pennsylvania GOP chair, on voting to censure Sen. Pat Toomey (R-PA) for his impeachment vote[4]

"The people sent me not to support his opinions, but to defend my own." Condorcet[5]

The recall is many things. Perhaps most surprisingly, it is a statement about a fundamental philosophical question on politics and how people want to be ruled. It is an answer to the above quotes – what do we expect from our elected officials? Are our elected officials' trustees, who are elected because of their own superior special talents, abilities or knowledge and, as such, are being trusted to make the best possible decisions for their constituents, even when those voters

Mark Baldassare, "What's Wrong with the Recall?" Public Policy Institute of California, July 28, 2021. https://www.ppic.org/blog/whats-wrong-with-the-recall/
Talmud Bavli, Baba Batra 12a. On the Sefaria website, it is translated as "A Sage is greater than a prophet" but others have translated it the way I did in the quote. Though this wouldn't be a political book if we didn't note that the comment is written by the wise men, not the prophets – or to cite comedian Emo Philips, "look who's telling me that."
KDKA, February 15,2021 twitter account as seen on "Quote of the Day:, Taegan Goddard's Political Wire, February 16, 2021, https://politicalwire.com/2021/02/16/quote-of-the-day-2810/
Clara Egger and Raul Magni-Berton, "The Recall in France: A Long Standing and Unresolved Debate" in The Politics of Recall Elections, 51

vehemently disagree with the decision? Or are they delegates, representatives or advocates,[6] elected because of their ability to successfully channel the views of these constituents to get the best possible policy? Essentially, are elected officials really advocates?

American history is a slow march to a more democratic system, one that over time has increasingly rejected the trustee model. We can see this trajectory in the rejection of a property requirement to vote; the quick failure of the original Electoral College model;[7] the move towards having voters choose the electors rather than the legislature; the Reconstruction Amendments expansion of the right to vote; the adoption of direct election of US Senators; the expansion of the franchise to women; the long-delayed Voting Rights Act and the lowering of the voting age; and the creation and triumph of the primary system rather than the caucus or party conventions to choose Presidents and other nominees. Direct democracy is a part of this same movement. It looks to give voters the right to create laws on their own and increases their ability to change officials.

The recall fits in to this framework, but it has always been the laggard of the direct democracy provisions – some even felt that it does not belong in that august category.[8] The first states adopted initiatives a decade before taking on the recall and initiatives have built a much more robust history. For example, Proposition 13 from 1978, which changed California's property tax laws, is believed to have reshaped the state's and possibly America's political landscape in ways that no recall has ever done. Initiatives are arguably responsible for two of the most groundbreaking developments in 21st Century America, the rapid acceptance of gay marriage and marijuana legalization. We cannot say any recall has had anywhere near the impact of these laws.

But with all that, the recall has managed to grab the spotlight again. Three high-profile recalls will have taken place this century. It has even broken through into the popular culture, both in a 2005 episode of *The Simpsons* and a 2013 plot line in *Parks & Recreation*.[9] Frankly, it may feel exactly right for our current environment. More than other electoral devices, the recall presents a stark choice.

It is not about potentially amorphous policy. It is instead deeply personal -- whether to kick a person out of office or not. The number of recalls may show that it is the recall's moment, at least on the state level. Since its reintroduction into American politics on the state level in 1908, only four governors and 39 state legislators will have faced a recall vote. Three of those four

---

[6] I did not create the Trustee/Representative divide idea. It goes back to Edmund Burke and John Stuart Mills. Note that Joseph Zimmerman, *The Recall: Tribunal of the People* (Westport: Praeger Publishers 1997) describes the same idea but uses the term delegate as interchangeable with Trustee. Instead of delegates/representatives/advocates, Zimmerman calls it the "agent concept." 4-5.

[7] I do have some specific thoughts on how the Electoral College was supposed to operate (and immediately failed) Joshua Spivak, The electoral college is a failure. The Founding Fathers would probably agree," *Washington Post*, April 7, 2019 and Joshua Spivak, "Stop Dreaming the Electoral College is here to stay," CNBC, December 13, 2016.

[8] Note the title of one of the premier organizations studying Direct Democracy: The Initiative and Referendum Institute.

[9] While Springfield may be in not another state, Parks & Recreations takes place in Indiana, one of the few states that does not allow the recall for any officials whatsoever.

governors have been in the last 18 years. Thirty-four of the state legislative recalls have taken place since 1981.

The Recall as the Bermuda Triangle:

There is an assumption that the recent spate of recalls serves as the start of a new role for the recall in electoral government as increasingly engaged - and enraged - voters insist on taking a more active role in policy making and that the recall is one of their best tools.
However, past successful recalls have not necessarily resulted in a boom. In fact, sometimes the opposite happens. After a prominent recall, changes in the law are frequently proposed, usually to no real effect, though Michigan's changes in 2012 did cut down on recalls in the state. But even without any legal changes, the recall has frequently gained enormous attention only to later disappear from view. In many ways, the recall is the Bermuda Triangle of politics.

My introduction to the academic side of the recall was an article with a footnote citing the dearth of writing on the recall.[10] That seems to be a theme with the recall, both in academia and in politics. The coverage of the subject, the long term trends, and even the basic history of the device quickly disappear from public view. In Arizona in 2011, the early reports of Senator Russell Pearce's recall couldn't even say for sure whether the state ever had a legislative recall.[11] Different reports claim that Michigan is tied for first in adopting the recall on the state-level in 1908.[12] Others, including contemporary sources, claim that the state didn't get around to it until 1913.[13]

We also have big historical questions about the subject. The recall was a topic for debate in the Ratification Conventions, but it wasn't included by Madison in the Amendments. After a couple of attempts to adopt the device, it was lost to headquarters until the end of the nineteenth century. Why did the recall disappear from view for over a century? Why? The concept of "Instructions for Senators", discussed below, was certainly a popular idea. So why was the recall forgotten?

Then, there is the harder question for us. Why did the recall fall out of favor so quickly after its reemergence? On the political front, the recall burned brightly during its adoption in the Progressive Era. But then, it disappeared from the scene. Between 1926 and 1975, the only state

---

[10] James Melcher, "Do they Recall?" *Comparative State Politics*, August 1996, 22, endnote 1. There was also Lawrence Sych. "State Recall Elections: What Explains Their Outcomes?" *Comparative State Politics* (October 1996). The Bermuda Triangle portion is so strong that not only can't I find the second article, I can't even find Comparative State Politics journal (or newsletter?) anywhere online.

[11] As befits this chapter, the link – and the newspaper is dead (and the Wayback Machine is no help). But it was in the *Tucson Citizen*, http://tucsoncitizen.com/arizona-news/2011/07/13/brewer-calls-nov-8-recall-election-for-pearce/

[12] National Conference of State Legislatures page, visited on July 28, 2021. https://www.ncsl.org/research/elections-and-campaigns/recall-of-state-officials.aspx

[13] This may be that 1913 is when the state adopted the provisions that allowed the recall to be used. Here's an article discussing Michigan's law, noting that the state adopted it in the constitution in 1908 see Jason Hanselman, "Total Recall: Balancing the Right to Recall Elected Officials with the Orderly Operation of Government," *Michigan Bar Journal*, January, 2014.http://www.michbar.org/file/journal/pdf/pdf4article2327.pdf, though this article from W.F. Dodd, "The Recall and the Political Responsibility of Judges," *Michigan Law Review*, December 1911, doesn't mention that Michigan is one of the states to have the provision. Bird & Ryan mention that the recall was adopted in 1913.

to add the recall was Alaska (in its new constitution). From 1935 to 1971, there were no state legislative recalls in the entire country. Why? We can throw out guesses (good economic climates, one-party domination, the power of local political organizations), but that's not a solid answer. It's not like the 1930s and 1960s didn't have plenty of political strife, but the recalls were not the weapon of choice to decide it. And then why did it return and stay active over the last 30 years?

There's also the judiciary, perhaps the most controversial of the recall issues. The now-esoteric topic of "recall of judicial decisions" played a large role in the 1912 election. But that subject disappeared off the map after an adverse Colorado Supreme Court ruling. Why did no one bring it back? And why have Judges so uniformly escaped the threat of the recall?

Today, the recall election has managed to take center stage. As we've seen in the past, this may be a temporary phenomenon. Or it may grow in import. So let's jump in:

Chapter 1: Playing the Odds -- How the Recall is Used

Over the last 10 years, I've tracked practically all the recalls that have taken place in the US. Most recall attempts or threats failed to get to the ballot. But of those that do go to a vote, they have been astonishingly successful.

From 2011-2020, I counted 1002 recalls that went to an election in the United States (when there are multiple officials facing recalls in one jurisdiction at once, I count each official separately as you must collect signatures for each individual). Additionally, 198 officials resigned in the face of recall threats or a recall election, plus 4 were removed by other means before the election could be held.[14]

601 were kicked out by the voters, 401 survived the vote – just about a 60% removal rate. These recalls took place in 29 states and the District of Columbia, plus an additional three states had officials resign in the face of recall threats. In California, recalls seem to take out about 78% of officials who face one.

The numbers represent more than a coin flip. One must compare this success rate to re-election rates. For all elected officials in America, there may be a 75-85 percent re-election rate. It is much higher in Congress, where we haven't seen a lower than 85 percent rate in many decades.[15] The recall flips the calculation on its head.

Chart 1 --- Recalls Over the Last 10 Years:

Year	Removed	Sustained (Kept in Office)	Resigned
2020	42	24	14
2019	37	34	16
2018	87	39	28
2017	39	29	31
2016	60	42	17
2015	66	28	15
2014	61	45	20
2013	51	35	22
2012	80	58	26
2011	78	67	9
Total	601	401	198

At least[16] 41 states have laws that allow recalls for some local officials, though the laws in some of these states are unclear and so limited that they effectively don't allow recalls. Nineteen states -- or perhaps 20, as Virginia's law is unclear -- allow the recall for some or all state-level

---

I have not included recalls in Native American Tribal Councils. There are a number of them, though they are very difficult to track.
Unfortunately, I cannot find the paper that lists the 75-85% re-election rate. Since 1964, Congress has had no election dip below 85%. OpenSecrets.org, https://www.opensecrets.org/elections-overview/reelection-rates
Every so often I find out that there is a state that seemingly doesn't allow recalls, but actually does (recently, I saw s with both New Hampshire and Vermont).

officials. Montana allows the recall against appointed officials.[17] Here is a breakdown of which states have the recall and whether it is allowed on the state-level or just limited to local officials

Chart 2 – State Breakdown on Recall Use:

State Level Recalls	Local Recalls Only	No Recalls
Alaska	Alabama	Delaware
Arizona	Arkansas	Indiana
California	Connecticut	Iowa
Colorado	District of Columbia	Kentucky
Georgia	Florida	Mississippi
Idaho	Hawaii	New York
Illinois (Only Governor on the state level)	Maine	Pennsylvania
Kansas	Maryland	South Carolina
Louisiana	Massachusetts	Utah
Michigan	Missouri	
Minnesota	Nebraska	
Montana	New Hampshire (still unclear)	
Nevada	New Mexico	
New Jersey	North Carolina	
North Dakota	Ohio	
Oregon	Oklahoma	
Rhode Island (Not the legislature)	South Dakota	
Virginia	Tennessee	

---

[17] A recent proposal in Illinois would have allowed the recall against legislative leaders, but it would have just removed them from the position, not the legislature itself. This provision was targeted at longtime House Speaker Mike Madigan.

Washington	Texas	
Wisconsin	Vermont	
	West Virginia	
	Wyoming	

Any look at recalls should start with the question of why people would want to launch a recall against an official. And beyond everything else we'll see here, the answer is easy: because they work.

Let's Define our Terms Gentlemen -- What is a Recall?

The entire history of the recall is filled with unclear and confusing terms, to such a degree that I've had to come up with my own terminology.

The problem jumps out at us right from the top: What is a recall? The term is used interchangeably for a number of different steps in the process.

A recall is an electoral procedure where petitioners collect signatures that allow them to get a new vote (or in one state, a trial) on whether the elected official should remain in office or not. There are variations that we will get into, but that's the basic idea.

But does a recall take place when:

1) petitions are taken out and signature gathering begins; or

2) when enough signatures get verified to have the official face the voters again; or

3) when that official is removed or retained by a vote?

I have regularly seen all of these variations used.

I use the term to refer to number 2, when the official faces a vote. For simplicity's sake, I recommend the first option should be called "facing recall petitions," even though that doesn't fit too nicely on a banner headline. Number three can be called either "recalled and removed" or "recalled and retained or sustained." This lets observers still see that the official faced the voters again and allows us to discern the results.

What is it called when a recall is used? The international literature likes the term "activation." We just call it a recall. What do you call an official who faces a recall vote and survives? A ecall survivor? Sustained in the position? Confusion reigns supreme.

Types of Recalls:

here are, and have always been, a huge assortment of recall laws. The early comprehensive study of the recall in California by Bird & Ryan notes that in the cities of California alone "…there has developed such a variety of treatment of all the features of the law that it is difficult to think of any possible innovation left untried."[18]

But the big divide is between what is referred to as Political Recalls and the Malfeasance Standard or Judicial Recall laws. It is here that we see the most common argument about recalls play out – should the recall be limited to actual misdeeds or should it be available for all types of actions?

Political Recalls are those that can be effectively launched for practically any reason whatsoever, the "I don't like your face" recalls. We see a lot of recalls for firing a city official, for approving development, for taxes, or for combining schools. All of these probably fall under a political recall law. Effectively, when you think of recalls – in California, Wisconsin, Colorado and the like -- political recalls are what we're talking about.

But there is a feeling, especially among editorial boards and people facing recalls, that the recall is really designed for use only in extreme cases of crimes or massive incompetence[19] or the catch-all term of malfeasance. Here's one editorial: "Recalls should be reserved for situations where elected officials are guilty of serious offenses – financial misconduct, ethical improprieties, continued offensive behavior, and unwillingness to carry out one's duties as an elected official and the like."[20] Or: "As a rule, California's institution of recall should be reserved to remove elected officials who are criminally corrupt or mentally ill. Occasionally, a recall is mounted when the motivation is about policy or the officeholder's behavior."[21]

Eight states constrain the recall law by requiring a statutorily delimitated list of violations that the targeted official must transgress before the recall is allowed to proceed (in all cases, the petitioners still have to gather the signatures).

Some of the literature calls this type of recall a "judicial recall" because either a judge or an election commissioner will have to rule as to whether the proposed recall meets the statutory requirement in order to proceed. Judicial recall is a confusing term as it is the same term that people use for a recall of a judge. Calling it a "for cause" recall is another option, though all recalls have a "cause" to them. I instead prefer the term "Malfeasance Standard" for this type of recall. It doesn't automatically infer criminal acts and it appears in some of the language of the laws. Not a perfect term, but then what is?

From this, we can see that the idea that recalls were designed solely for misbehavior is clearly

---

[18] Frederick L. Bird and Frances Ryan, The Recall of Public Officers: A Study of the Operation of the Recall in California, New York: The Macmillan Co. 1930) , 58

[19] I only know of one case that seemed to be focused on incompetence. In 2011 in Kansas, Shawnee County Treasurer Larry Wilson was accused of commingling funds from motor vehicle and real estate taxes and not developing written emergency exit procedures for staff. Both parties called for his ouster. Petitioners need 31,395 signatures, so they didn't get enough to get on the ballot. Tim Hrenchir, "Effort to recall Wilson taken to courthous steps," Topeka Capital-Journal, January 3, 2012.

[20] "Recall isn't the Proper Response," Norfolk Daily News, November 7, 2015.

[21] Dick Spotwood, "Glickman Could Avoid Recall Effort by Running Again," Marin Independent Journal, June 1 2019.

wrong. The result is that policy battles or political efforts are normally the focus of recalls, though the political dimension does not necessarily mean they are partisan. Frequently, they are intraparty fights. How likely is a recall over criminal or malfeasance actions? Among the 39 state legislative recalls as well as the gubernatorial ones, only four can truly be considered to have been launched for potentially criminal actions: California in 1913, Oregon in 1985 and 1988 and Wisconsin in 2003.

Political recalls predate the malfeasance standard ones. With one very unclear exception, all the early states adopted political recall laws. I am not sure when malfeasance standard recalls came into being. Kansas, which adopted a recall in 1912, has such a law. But it took until the 1970s for the state's legislature to put in place laws that allowed the recall to be used. It may be that Alaska is the first state to have adopted a real malfeasance standard, and it is one that has been fought over ever since – and may now be at an end.[22]

There have been attempts to change laws from allowing Political Recalls to limiting recalls to Malfeasance Standard ones. After the Wisconsin recalls in 2011-2012, future Speaker of the Assembly Robin Vos proposed just such a move, however nothing came of it. Michigan made some changes, notably a factualness and clarity requirement, but it is still clearly a political recall state. The Newsom recall is also leading to calls to adopt a Malfeasance Standard to ward off future recalls. The one jurisdiction that I know changed the law was College Station, Texas in 2012.[23]

The big takeaway here is that when you are looking at a recall, it is probably a political recall. If you live in a state with a Malfeasance Standard/Judicial Recall law, there has to be some good cause according to a judge for the recall.

The Voting Forms of Recall Elections:

The recall effort against Governor Gavin Newsom (D) has brought attention to the way the recall actually operates and whether it is "fair."

California's recall law uses a one-day, two-step process. There is a binary, up or down vote on whether Newsom should stay or go, where he needs to win a majority (or a tie) to stay in office. At the same election, voters also cast a concurrent vote on the replacement candidate, which counts if Newsom loses.[24] The replacement candidate only needs a plurality of the replacement vote to be elected – in this case, that may be about 2.17%, not including people who ignore the replacement question. Newsom is not allowed to run to replace himself. The result of this structure is that Newsom's replacement can win office with a tiny fraction of the vote that

---

[22] Alaska's Supreme Court has repeatedly cut back the limits on the law. A recent Supreme Court decision allowing he recall of Governor Mike Dunleavy to move forward may have effectively turned the state into a Political Recall ate.

[3] "College Station voters approve changes to city charter," *The Eagle,* November 7, 2012. It was Proposition 1 and assed overwhelmingly – 15,000 –3,590.

[⁴] In the 2003 recall, there was a lawsuit over whether people who did not vote on the recall question could only oted on the replacement candidate (the law said they effectively could not). The Court held the provision as nconstitutional and you can just vote on the replacement. *Partnoy v. Shelley*, 277 F.Supp. 2d 1063 (SD Cal. 2003). tps://casetext.com/case/partnoy-v-shelley-2

Newsom received in losing office.

Despite the fact that there were 135 candidates on the replacement ballot, Arnold Schwarzenegger received almost 200,000 more votes in the replacement race than Gray Davis/No on Recall received. But over the last 10 years, there have been at least five instances where the elected official who was kicked out in the recall outdrew the winner of the replacement race, including the most recent state-level recall election, California State Senator Josh Newman in 2018.

The issue of whether a recall victor should be able to receive fewer votes than the removed official is not new, though it only recently has become the source of significant controversy, with the a law dean claiming that it is "Unconstitutional" based on a rather novel interpretation of key Supreme Court cases like Baker v. Carr and Reynolds v. Sims (the one person, one vote decisions that required districts for legislative elections to be relatively even-sized by population).[25] While we will see that the courts are generally not fans of the recall, it seems like it would be a quite a stretch to declare it unconstitutional on these grounds.

Recall laws across the country have seen attempts to solve the problem of how to choose a new candidate. Idaho uses what I call a "Queen of the Hill" provision (the amount of votes in favor of the recall has to top the votes received by the official in their victory).[26]

Some local jurisdictions, as well as many countries, require an "absentee veto" – where total voter turnout in a recall needs to be higher than a set percentage of the population in order for the recall to count. In 2012, the President of Romania survived due to a 46% turnout, as opposed to the 50% required. The Mayor of Warsaw similarly beat back a recall in 2013, where turnout needed to be 29.1% and was instead 25.66%.[27] Others require a supermajority of the vote in order for the official to be ousted. In Tennessee, where recalls are only allowed on the local level, some jurisdictions require that 66% of the voters cast their ballot for removal in order for the official to be ousted.

In the 19 (or possibly 20) states in the US that allow recalls against Governors or state level officials, the primary divisions in recall structure are:

1) Yes or No vote on the official or just a new election;
2) Replacement race or filling the position in the matter set out by the law (i.e. the Lieutenant Governor takes over);
3) Whether a replacement race should be on the same day as the recall or held on a different day.

---

[25] Erwin Chermerinsky and Aaron S. Edlin, "There Is a Problem with California's Recall. It's Unconstitutional." *New York Times*, August 11, 2021.
[26] James V. Saturno, "Queen of the Hill Rules in the House of Representatives," *Congressional Research Services,* September 24, 2015. https://budgetcounsel.files.wordpress.com/2016/11/rs20313.pdf
[27] ""Train Basescu likely to stay as Romanian president," *Global Times*, July 30, 2012. https://www.globaltimes.cn/content/724131.shtml "Warsaw Mayor survives recall vote after too low turnout," *Radio Poland,* October 12, 2013. http://archiwum.thenews.pl/1/9/Artykul/149987,Warsaw-mayor-survives-recall-vote-after-too-low-turnout

Chart 3: Recall Election Procedure by State:

Yes or No Vote + Same Day Replacement Race	Yes or No Vote + Different Day Replacement Vote	Yes or No Vote + Replacement decided by law (i.e. Lt. Gov. steps up)	New Elections
California	Georgia	Alaska	Arizona
Colorado	Illinois (though primary could be the same day)	Idaho	Nevada (if no other candidate runs, yes or no vote)
	Louisiana	Kansas	North Dakota
	Minnesota	Michigan (only for the governor, all others use New Election)	Wisconsin (with primaries)
	Montana	Oregon (No Lt. Gov., Secretary of State steps up)	
	New Jersey	Washington	
	Rhode Island		

Recall Trial: Virginia (probably doesn't impact the Governor, may hit other state officials).

Even within these divisions, there are variations. In some places, candidates are allowed to run in the replacement race, which has led to the odd result of a candidate being defeated and then replacing themselves (we'll see this later under local recall laws). Some states, like Wisconsin, limit recalls to one per term or one per a set time period. Other jurisdictions have no limit whatsoever. East Cleveland Councilman Thomas Wheeler faced three recalls in a year, winning two before being ousted in December 2016.

The Yes or No with a new election may seem unfair, but the most recent states to adopt the recall (Illinois, Minnesota, New Jersey, Rhode Island, Georgia and Montana) have all opted for this method with a replacement race.

States have also changed their laws over time. Oregon moved to the automatic replacement model (actually, filling the replacement by law rather than election) in the early years of having the recall; Michigan made this change for Governor back in 2012. During the Newsom recall, there has been discussion of changing California's law to one of the other method, most specifically the Lieutenant Governor replacement model. This limits the political value of the recall, but also may make it theoretically more likely to result in a recall, especially if the two officials are from different parties (as was the case for 20 straight years, between 1978-1998). This way, there is a guarantee that the other party will capture the seat in the case of a recall. It seems unlikely, but it is certainly in the realm of possibilities.

Shocker: Special Elections vs. General/Primary Elections

My long-standing assumption has been that one reason that recalls are so successful is that they frequently take place as a special election rather than on the same day as a general or primary election. The logic is once again clear: The Movers' Advantage. The recall is launched by angry, motivated voters who are coming out to play, and they favor the recall. The official being targeted has to alert their own supporters to get turnout up. Everyone I've spoken to believes this as a rule.

Welp, wrong! Recalls taking place on the same day as a general or primary election seem to be only slightly more likely to oust the official than one that takes place on a special election day.[28] A little over 60% of recalls take place on a special election day. Slightly less than 40% take place on the same day as a primary or a general election. To my everlasting shock, the contemporaneous elections are more likely to result in a removal. Special elections lead to a removal in about 58% of the recall votes. General or Primary Election Day recalls lead to removal in 64%.

Chart 4: Special Elections v. General Election Results

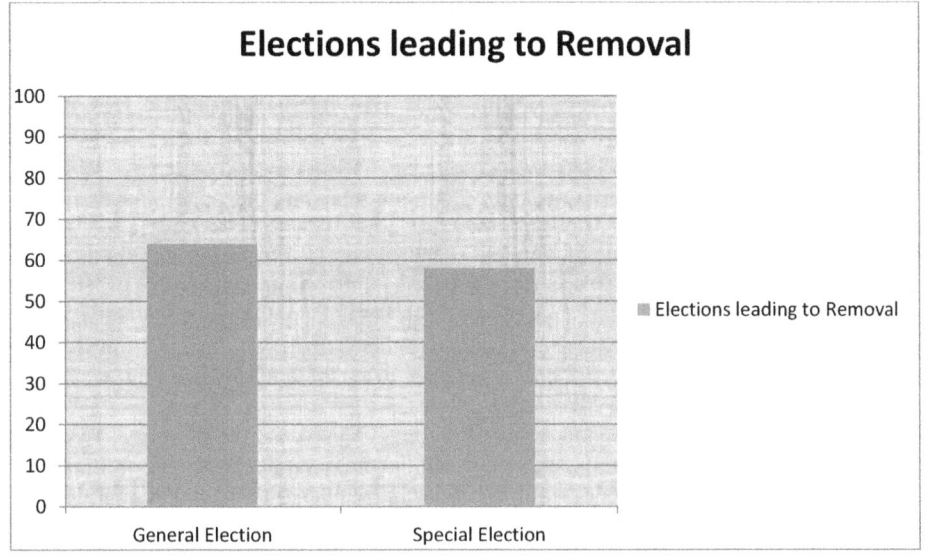

---

[28] Joshua Spivak, "The Myth of Special Elections,' *Governing Magazine,* June 3, 2019. In a different vein, I look how special elections might not work out well for appointed US Senators, Joshua Spivak, "The Perils of Special Election," *Washington Post,* December 18, 2008.

What explains this? I don't know that there is anything except that the numbers are pretty close together and perhaps it doesn't matter at all. Quite the surprise.

The exchange: Longer terms in office

As mentioned above, terms of office were frequently shorter in the past, with many governors serving two year terms. At times, one of the justifications for adopting the recall has been that it can be paired with longer terms of office, thereby giving concerned voters an out.

Historian Rod Farmer notes that "It was common for progressives to argue for the recall as something that would allow for longer terms in office and shorter ballots." Farmer notes that progressive historian Charles Beard said "the possibility of lengthening the terms of public officers, a thing highly desirable for the sake of efficient administration, will doubtlessly commend the recall to the consideration of many,,,,"[29]

Rhode Island, one of the most recent states to adopt the recall, used this exact reason in passing its referendum. The bill, passed in 1992, was explicitly titled "Four Year Terms and Recall Provisions for State Officers." The voters approved this law (which is just for state-wide officials and exempts the legislature – the first state to do that). Was the recall important for the term expansion? Look back a little and we see that there was an attempt in 1973 to go to four year terms without the recall, but it was voted down. [30]

In 1932, Arkansas voters rejected an initiative that would have increased terms and (among other provisions) added a recall. The initiative was shot down by voters (Arkansas had previously adopted a recall law, but we'll get to that soon enough).

We can see that term expansion was considered in adopting the recall. The first paper looking at Oregon's adoption and use of the recall, written in 1915, draws as one of its conclusions:

"But the terms of office in Oregon are now generally too short, and the adoption of the recall has opened the way for an increase in the length of terms – an important reform apparently otherwise impossible."[31]

We see this in Wisconsin as well, as an op-ed from William Evuje from the Capital Times in 1951, states: "A good argument might be made for the four-year term if we had an effective recall system in Wisconsin," he wrote. "Without this, the people would be stuck for four years without recourse if a bad governor was elected."[32]

Rod Farmer, "Power to the People: The Progressive Movement for the Recall, 1890s-1920." *The New England Journal of History*, Winter 2001, 59-83. 16 (on this site) http://www.iandrinstitute.org/docs/Farmer-Recall.pdf
Patrick T. Conley and Robert G. Flanders Jr., The Rhode Island Constitution, Oxford University Press, 2011. 153. Also, the vote is here https://elections.ri.gov/elections/results/1992/referenda.php/ Also see this story on how Common Cause in Rhode Island looked to pair the increased term with a recall. "Vermont and Rhode Island Debate Length of Their Governors' Terms," *New York Times*. February 19, 1991.
James Barnett, *The Operation of the Initiative, Referendum and Recall in Oregon* (New York: Macmillian, 1915), Once again, I can't find this and just have the original link that now is dead: William Evuje, "Capital Times, p://host.madison.com/ct/news/local/writers/jack_craver

Chapter 2: Origin Stories

Greeks, Romans, Colonial Times and the Constitutional Convention

The recall is a device whose origins are unsettled. The man widely seen as its modern day creator, Dr. John Randolph Haynes, claimed that it was "derived historically from Greek and Latin sources...."[33] and other scholars have found forms of recalls in Greece, Rome and Poland.[34] Some cite Switzerland for its modern incarnation (the Swiss also get credit for the initiative and referendum).[35]

For the United States, the recall's origins trace back through to the beginning of colonial history. The laws of the General Court of the Massachusetts Bay Colony, adopted in 1631, called for the election of Assistants[36] and a provision that they "shall see cause for any defect or misbehavior to remove any one or more of the Assistants."[37] The Massachusetts charter of 1691 also said that "Councillors or Assistants or any of them shall or may at any time hereafter be removed or displaced from their respective Places or Trusts."[38]

This form of the recall involved the removal of an official by another elected body, such as a state legislature recalling its United States senator. While this form provides a different relationship between the elected official and the general population than does the modern recall, the principles and the debates that engulfed the issue have not substantially changed.

The recall gained a firm footing in American politics with the democratic ideals that burst forth from the American Revolution. After declaring their independence, 11 of the 13 colonies wrote new constitutions, and many of these documents showed the new spirit of democracy. Most lessened the power of the executive and strengthened the legislature. Some opened up the right to vote to a larger portion of the population. And a few states wrote the recall into law as a method of exercising control over their elected representatives.

The states which adopted the recall were mainly concerned with the power of the representatives who served the states in the national government's congress. Pennsylvania's constitution of 1776 said that "any delegate (to the Continental Congress) may be superseded at any time, by the General Assembly appointing another in his stead." Vermont adopted the same language in their 1777 constitution.[39]

---

[33] Dr. John Randolph Haynes. Direct Government in California. Address read at the National Popular Government League July 5 and 6, 1916. Senate Document No. 738. 4.

[34] Matt Qvortrup, "The Political Theory of the Recall. A Study in the History of the Ideas," in The Politics of Recall Elections, 2020, 30-32. It is mentioned in Plutarch as occurring in the third century B.C.

[35] See Thomas E. Cronin, Direct Democracy: The Politics of Initiative, Referendum and Recall, Harvard University Press, 1989 and Laura Tallian, Direct Democracy, (Los Angeles: People's Press, 1977) 13-15.

[36] "The magistrates who came to constitute the upper branch of the Legislature." Robert Luce, Legislative Principles (Boston: Riverside Press, 1930) 488.

[37] Ibid. 488.

[38] The Federal and State Constitutions Colonial Charters, and other Organic Laws of the States Territories and Colonies now or heretofore forming The United States of America, Ed. Francis Thorpe, (Washington, D.C.: Government Printing Press, 1906), 1879.

[39] Thorpe. Constitutions, 3085, 6578.

The revolution's success led the states to form the weak government under the Articles of Confederation, which was at the mercy of the individual states. It is therefore not surprising that the states incorporated the provisions of the recall into the Articles of Confederation.[40] According to John Lansing (later a proponent of the recall at the New York State Ratifying Convention), the recall was never exercised by any of the states throughout the history of the Confederation.[41]

The Articles of Confederation government only lasted a few years before the next step in America's political evolution came about. Without hyperbole, the 1787 Constitutional Convention in Philadelphia is likely the single most fascinating intellectual political event in US history, one that has seen the debates surrounding its adoption, and its eventual impact endlessly analyzed. Yet the issue of the recall – which was present at the Convention exactly in its modern form -- has been mostly ignored.

The recall was proposed by Virginia Governor Edmund Randolph in his presentation of the Virginia Plan on May 29 (probably written by James Madison). The plan would have allowed the recall of members of the first house of the legislature, who were directly elected by the people.[42] On June 12, the convention passed Charles Pinckney's motion to strike out the practice, along with a ban on re-election for the members of the first house.[43] Madison's notes have no explanation why this happened. The recall then disappeared from view for almost the entire convention, only coming back during a speech by Elbridge Gerry, which explored how the convention exceeded its mandate by contrasting some of the differences between the proposed Constitution and the Articles of Confederation.[44]

While the Convention may have ignored it, the lack of a recall for US Senators was a rallying point for the anti-Constitution group – the anti-Federalists. One of the major opponents of the Constitution at the Convention, Luther Martin, stressed the lack of the recall, and the freedom from popular control that this absence represented, as a reason to reject the document. He played a role of anti-Federalist intellectual leader, one similar to the Federalist positions of James Madison, Alexander Hamilton and James Wilson.[45]

Martin was opposed to granting Senators, who were seen as representing the more traditional aristocratic population, a large degree of freedom. He feared that Senators would disregard their position as delegates of the people, and be free to work against the interests of their own states.

---

[40] Articles of Confederation, Article V. For the more convenient management of the general interests of the United States, delegates shall be annually appointed in such manner as the Legislature of each State shall direct, to meet in Congress on the first Monday in every year, with a power reserved to each State to recall its delegates, or any of them, at any time within the year, and to send others in their stead, for the remainder of the year.
[41] The Debates in the Several State Conventions on the Adoption of the Federal Constitution by the General Convention at Philadelphia in 1787, Ed. Jonathan Elliot. Philadelphia: J.J. Lippincott Company, 1891. 2:299-300.
[42] Debates. 5:127
[43] Ibid. 5:185. Also to be found here: https://avalon.law.yale.edu/18th_century/debates_612.asp
[44] Debates. 5:422. Gerry was one of the delegates who refused to sign the constitution. The future VP under Madison is now best remembered (and unfairly tarnished) for giving his name to the Gerrymander. Unlike our pronunciation, Gerry's name had a hard G.
[45] Little remembered today, James Wilson, unlike Hamilton, appears to be one of the major figures of the Constitutional Convention. If you are thinking of Hamilton's role in Philadelphia (due to his yeoman's work in the ratification fight), the part was probably played by Wilson.

Martin said: "Thus, sir, for six years, the senators are rendered totally and absolutely independent of their states, of whom they ought to be the representatives, without any bond or tie between them."[46]

The idea of tightly binding the senators to their states was strongly opposed by the Federalists, most notably Alexander Hamilton. The topic took up several days of debate in the New York Ratifying Convention and was also proposed in the Massachusetts Convention. Hamilton was in the lead in his unyielding opposition to burdening senators with the fear of a recall. In an echo of later fights, while Martin and John Lansing[47] argued for the officials to act as delegates, Hamilton wanted them to have the freedom to make statesmanlike choices. In the same argument that opponents of the recall would make more than a century later, Hamilton feared that the recall "will render the senator a slave to all the capricious humors among the people."[48]

In New York on June 24, 1788, towards the end of the ratification debates, Gilbert Livingston introduced a measure calling for the recall of senators by state legislatures, and limit senators to serving no more than 6 years out of any 12. Livingston was concerned that states would have "little or no check" on senators who have a six year term of office.[49] Lansing described the senate as "a kind of bulwark to the independence of the states, and a check to the encroachment of the general Government..."[50] If this precaution was not taken, Lansing said: "they will lose their respect for the power from whom they receive their existence, and consequently disregard the great object for which they are instituted."[51]

This point of view met with strong resistance from the proponents of the Constitution. Chancellor Robert Livingston argued that "the Senate are indeed designed to represent the state governments; but they are also the representatives of the United States, and are not to consult the interest of any one state but that of the Union. This could never be done, if there was a power of recall; for sometimes it happens that small sacrifices are absolutely indispensable for the good and safety of the confederacy."[52]

Hamilton denied the premise that the state legislatures would be more in tune with the will of the people. He argued that the recall would prevent the senators from being able to make difficult decisions. Hamilton said:

Without attempting to prove that the legislatures must be, in a great degree, the image of the multitude, in respect to federal affairs, and that the same prejudices and factions will prevail, I insist that, in whatever body the power of recall is vested, the senator will perpetually feel

---

[46]Jonathan Elliot. The Debates in the several State Conventions on the Adoption of the Federal Constitution by the General Convention at Philadelphia in 1787 Philadelphia: J.J. Lippincott Company, 1891. 1:361
[47]Lansing was a New York delegate to the Philadelphia convention, which he left early because he felt the delegates had exceeded their mandate.
[48]Alexander Hamilton, The Papers of Alexander Hamilton, Ed. Harold Syrett. (New York: Columbia Univ. Press, 1962) 5:69.
[49]Elliot. 2:288.
[50]New York State Convention, The Debates and Proceedings of the convention of the state of New York, (New York: Francis Childs, 1788) 63
[51]Elliot. 2:289.
[52]Elliot. 2:291

imself in such a state of vassalage and dependence, that he never can posses that firmness hich is necessary to the discharge of his great duty to the Union.[53]

ew York finally voted to ratify the Constitution, but there were still attempts to bring up rious amendments. Rhode Island, the last state to ratify in 1790, proposed 21 amendments, cluding granting state legislatures the "power to recall" their federal senators.[54] The recall of nators came up twice more, as the legislature in Virginia attempted to bring the topic up as a nstitutional amendment in 1803 and 1808. The 1808 amendment was met by resolutions of sapproval from six states.[55]

ith the Federalists' victory, the recall went into hibernation. Recent failed court cases seeking allow the recall of US Senators have looked to a letter from George Washington, written to his phew Bushrod Washington, which they claim show he supported a recall law for senators.[56] owever, this has been rejected by the courts.

here were still attempts to exercise power over senators. State legislatures tried to claim the wer of Instruction – where they could send instructions to the senators who should follow em... or not. The Instructions did not have the power of law (though some senators resigned in e face of Instructions).[57] Instructions had their big moment in the 1830s Whigs vs. Jacksonian emocrats fight and antebellum period and faded after that.[58] was not until the country was faced with a very different set of circumstances that the recall -emerged as a viable political option. By that time, the field of debate had shifted to the state vel, with the people themselves possessing the power of the recall. But the focus of the debates d the nature of the arguments remained the same.

How a Resurrection Really Feels[59] -- The Recall Returns:

fter failing to get into the Constitution, the recall fell completely off the map until the late 19th d early 20th Century. It's not clear why it disappeared and why it came back. The best we can y is that the return was part of the Progressive Movement. Without getting into too much depth out the ill-defined and, (to our eyes) occasionally contradictory policies of the progressives,

---

lliot. 2:303
lliot, Debates. 1:337 Amendment XVIII.
uce. 490.
"The power under the Constitution will always be in the People. It is entrusted for certain defined purposes... and enever it is executed contrary to their Interest, or not agreeable to their wishers, their Servants can, and doubtedly will be, recalled." Letter from George Washington to Bushrod Washington, November 10, 1987. This quoted in the briefs of both the New Jersey and North Dakota Supreme Court decisions barring recalls of nators. https://www.ndcourts.gov/supreme-court/dockets/20100228/18. I would argue that this shows the lack of rity of the term "recall."
See Clement Eaton, "Southern Senators and the Right of Instruction, 1789-1860," The Journal of Southern story, Vol. 18, No. 3, August 1952, 303-319 for a great look at Instruction.
Eaton, 319. "The doctrine of the right of legislative instruction became obsolete after 1860. It had matured in a riod of great political partisanship during which the two-party system was emerging. Although in theory the trine of instruction seemed to be a noble expression of representative government, in actual practice it was ject to dangerous abuses which thoroughly discredited it."
'm aware of the irony of citing The Hold Steady, whose lyrics in "Two-Handed Handshake" specifically make of this.

their focus was on cleaning up the moral and political health of the country. As opponents of "big" – both political bosses and business monopolies -- the progressives were proponents of delegating power to the populace, including women's suffrage, primaries, the Australian (or secret) ballot, direct election of Senators and Direct Democracy or Direct Legislation laws.

Considered "the chief political legacy of state progressivism,"[60] direct democracy has been adopted in the majority of American states. Twenty-six states provide for the initiative or popular referendum[61] (and, as mentioned, 41 allow the recall of some officials).

For a long time, the recall was believed to have reappeared on the scene in the 1892 and 1896 platforms of the Socialist-Labor Party and the Populist Party,[62] where it was sometimes called the "imperative mandate" (though the imperative is a little different than the recall as shown in the note).[63] However, mainstream backers of the direct democracy movement did not support the recall. Eltweed Pomeroy, President of the National Direct Legislation League, argued against the recall because it "involves the personal element in a manner allowing for reprisals and political revenge." The recall was not part of the platform at the 1896 Convention of the Direct Legislation League.[64] In 1898, when South Dakota became the first state to adopt the initiative and referendum, the recall was nowhere to be found, and it was also absent from other states that subsequently adopted direct democracy.[65] It took a Philadelphia-born Doctor in Los Angeles to truly revive the recall.

Or maybe it didn't. Most credit Dr. John Randolph Haynes with bringing it back in Los Angeles in 1903, though Thomas Cronin mentions in his book Direct Democracy that other small California jurisdictions had it first.[66] I asked Cronin, but he did not remember the cities. However, in July 2021, Gerry Cohen, a North Carolina Wake County Election Board Member (and Duke Law School Adjunct Instructor) discovered that San Diego had the provision in their charter in 1889.[67] So thanks to Cohen's find, we may be able to push the recall law's return back more than 20 years. Since this is missing from all contemporary accounts, including the Bird &

---

[60]Thomas K. McCraw, "The Progressive Legacy" in The Progressive Era, Lewis Gould, ed., (New York: Syracuse Univ. Press, 1974), 185.

[61]The Initiative and Referendum Institute at http://www.iandrinstitute.org/statewide_i&r.htm. The popular referendum is different than the legislative referenda, which allows voters to approve legislative acts. Every state has the legislative referenda in some fashion (except perhaps Delaware).

[62]National Party Platforms 1840-1972, compiled by Donald Bruce Johnson and Kirk H. Porter (Urbana: Univ. of Illinois Press,1973), 96. Zimmerman,The Recall, 9.

[63] The Imperative, which tracks back to Rome, medieval Europe and the 1871 French Commune, operates differently than the recall. Under the imperative, the elected officials are given specific instructions and can be removed if they don't follow them. In some ways, this is similar to the old US idea of Instructions for Senators. European Commission For Democracy Through Law, Report on the Imperative Mandate and similar Practices (3. 14, 2009). https://www.venice.coe.int/webforms/documents/default.aspx?pdffile=CDL-AD(2009)027-e

[64] Thomas Sitton, John Randolph Haynes: California Progressive (Stanford: Stanford University Press, 199. 35-3

[65] Before Oregon approved the state-level recall in 1908, South Dakota, Utah (1900), Oregon (1902), Nevada (1904), Montana (1906), Oklahoma (1907), Maine (1908) and Missouri (1908) all accepted some of the other direct democracy provisions. Cronin, Direct Democracy, 51.

[66] Cronin, Direct Democracy. Hat tip to Rod Farmer for pointing this out to me.

[67] Charter of the City of San Diego, Adopted March 16, 1889 at https://www.sandiego.gov/sites/default/files/legacy/city-clerk/pdf/archives/1889a.pdf. I found out about it from an article discussing recalls in North Carolina, which (to my shock) cited Cohen talking about San Diego (which, to shock, was an amazing historical find). The recall provision is on page 11.

Ryan book, this is truly a mystery, and calls into question some of the history. Did Haynes know that San Diego had a recall law? Why didn't he or anyone else cite it? I wish I had an answer here, but that'll have to wait for future research.

Back to our time frame, Oregon, under noted reformer William U'Ren, became the first state to adopt the recall for state-level officials in 1908. The vote, which took place a decade after the adoption of the initiative, was viewed as the "final crowning act to complete the temple of popular government...."[68]

Oregon kicked off a wave of adoptions.

Chart 5: Adoption of the recall by state with voting percentage

Year:	State:	Vote:
1908	Oregon	65%
1908	Michigan	Part of a new Constitution
1911	California	76%
1912	Arizona	81.4%
1912	Arkansas (Ruled Unconstitutional)	55%
1912	Colorado	57.5%
1912	Idaho	73.7%
1912	Nevada	89%
1912	Washington	70.7%
1914	Kansas	64%
1914	Louisiana	75%
1920	North Dakota	63%
1926	Wisconsin	50.6%
1959	Alaska	Part of the Constitution
1976	Montana	57%
1978	Georgia	68.3%
1992	Rhode Island	60%
1995	New Jersey	76%
1996	Minnesota	88.05%
2010	Illinois	65.9%

Starting with Alaska in 1959, most of the states that have adopted the recall have severely limited its use, either through a Malfeasance Standard and/or through other means. Only New Jersey among those states has a political recall law, though one with a very high barrier to get on the ballot (25% of turnout). The earlier states all seem to have adopted a form of the political recall law, though courts and others have pushed Georgia, Kansas and Washington to a Malfeasance Standard.

[James] Barnett, *The Operation of the Initiative, Referendum and Recall in Oregon* (New York: Macmillian, 1915), 89.

In nearly all the states, the recall was approved by voters, frequently overwhelmingly. As far as I know, only three states have had the recall go to the ballot and vote it down. But we need a pretty big asterisk.

As we'll see in greater detail below, Wisconsin voted down a recall law in 1914 (along with measures proposing ballot initiatives) in an election repudiating progressives. However, the state later adopted a recall in 1926.

Arkansas voters actually passed a recall law in the first set of initiatives allowed back in 1912. The State Supreme Court quickly quashed the recall, ruling that the initiative law limited voters to three ballot measures per election. There were nine measures, although only three of them were approved. The state-wide recall was tossed out and has not returned.

In 1932, Arkansas voters rejected an amendment that included the recall. However, the recall was a tacked-on portion of a larger amendment, one that looked to provide a split legislative session and increase the term of office for state officials to four years. As part of the deal for the longer term, state officials would have been subject to recall. This measure went down to defeat, along with seven other initiatives. Arkansas has discussed adopting a recall since, but with the tight three measure limit, the recall never seems to make the cut. Still, Arkansas has used the recall at lower levels of government.

Nebraska and Utah are the only two states that I know to have straight out rejected a recall law and never brought it back. In 1938, Nebraska rejected the recall amendment.[69] In 1976, the Utah Recall and Advisory Recall Act went down to defeat by a tiny margin, 254,866 – 257,246.[70]

Utah has since discussed adopting a recall law, especially one targeting Senator Mitt Romney after he voted in favor of impeachment, but nothing has come of it.

Rather than get into the details on every states' adoption of the recall (which I don't have – though this note looks a little into the Western nature of the recall),[71] let us look at the adoption in two states that provide the most interesting examples. Let's start by seeing how the fabled and

---

[69]"Official Tally Shows that 505,471 Voted in Election," The Lincoln Star, November 29, 1938. The vote was 42% in favor of the recall 124,829-170,863. Oddly, many voters skipped the question.

[70] https://elections.utah.gov/Media/Default/Documents/Election_Results/General/1976Gen.pdf

[71] You'll notice that all the states west of the Mississippi have the recall, save for Utah. I believe this has to do with the political dynamic inherent in later developing states. The East Coast had already developed a political system with competing interests, while the West did not, allowing for an overarching power to gain control in the state. Note this comment on why the recall is so rare in the South: "There are several possible explanations for why the South did not adopt these new direct democracy techniques. The labor movement, which supported initiative and referendum with greater enthusiasm, was weaker in the South than elsewhere in the country. Widespread illiteracy in the South and white fear of black domination may have been restraints on the adoption of some form of direct democracy. Although the drive for the initiative and referendum often 'united the reform impulses of the urban lab movement with those of the rural Populist farmers,' the South was not interested." Calvin R. Ledbetter, Jr. "Adoption of Initiative and Referendum in Arkansas: The Roles of George W. Donaghey and William Jennings Bryan," The Arkansas Historical Quarterly, Vol. 51, No. 3 (1992) 199-223, 202. David Schmidt, Citizen Lawmakers (Philadelphia, 1989) 13, 7.

feared Southern Pacific Railroad – "the Octopus" -- got us here.

California: Riding the Rails

The driving of the Golden Spike completing the intercontinental railroad represented a radical change in political life in California.[72] The state would now be controlled by the railroads, most prominent among them the Southern Pacific Railroad (popularly known as the "Espee" or "SP").[73] Fremont Older, an anti-railroad leader, explained the bi-partisan nature of this domination:

There was only one kind of politics and that was corrupt politics. It didn't matter whether a man was a Republican or a Democrat. The Southern Pacific Railroad controlled both parties, and he either had to stay out of the game altogether or play it with the railroad.[74]

With its massive wealth and monopoly on the fastest means of shipping and travel, the Southern Pacific was able to swat away all comers.

After years of battle, the insurgent progressives began making progress against the Espee. One of their leaders was a physician and Philadelphia transplant, Dr. John Randolph Haynes, who formed the Direct Legislation League of Los Angeles in 1900.

Los Angeles was no stranger to direct democracy. In 1898, in a failed attempt to revise the city's charter, the Board of Freeholders approved an initiative and referendum, but rejected the recall proposal.[75] Another attempt to revise the charter saw the creation of a fifteen-member committee in 1900. Haynes won election to this committee. Haynes proposed the initiative, referendum and recall to combat the "[I]nefficiency, extravagance and corruption [which] characterise the management of city affairs,"[76] The Board of Freeholders approved all three provisions, though not without opposition.[77] Haynes' friendship with (and role as personal physician) of *Los Angeles Times* publisher Harrison Gray Otis led the conservative paper to cautiously support the recall – (this friendship would end badly and the LA Times became a leading opponent of the recall).[78] The recall was approved with a four to one vote in favor.[79]

The recall quickly got a work-out, with the removal of Councilman James Davenport in 1904

---

[72] How different was California before this? In 1859, California Supreme Court Chief Justice David Terry shot and killed Senator David Broderick in a duel. Thirty years later, Terry was killed by the bodyguard of US Supreme Court Justice Stephen Field after Terry assaulted Field.
[73] Sitton, 85. Also see "Espee Directors Meet," *Los Angeles Times*, (September 7, 1900) for example of the use of the term "Espee."
[74] Fremont Older, My Own Story (New York: MacMillian Co., 1926), 176-177.
[75] Sitton, *John Randolph Haynes,* 36.
[76] *Los Angeles Times* (September 29, 1900).
[77] Board of Freeholder member Sherman Page said "it would be an experiment for which no necessity exists." "Initiative and Referendum: Freeholders Adopt Those and a Recall Clause – Latter was Opposed." *Los Angeles Times*, (October 10, 1900). Haynes was able to fight off this opposition.
[78] Here is where the LAT used the nickname "The Grand Bounce" – a personal favorite. See Sitton, *John Randolph Haynes,* at 41 for use of the term "Grand Bounce."
[79] See Bird and Ryan, *The Recall of Public Officers ,*27-28, for why the charter took several years to be approved.

and Mayor Arthur "A.C." Harper in 1909.[80] About twenty-five other California localities adopted the device in short order.

But the larger battle in the state was still being fought. Formed in 1862, the California Constitution of 1879 cemented the Southern Pacific's role as an "octopus" in the words of a best-selling novel, able to penetrate its tentacles everywhere.[81] Historian George Mowry noted that the Espee's power was unusual: "To a degree perhaps unparalleled in the nation, the Southern Pacific and a web of associated economic interests ruled the state."[82]

Recent historians have taken a more nuanced assessment of this power, describing the railroad as less monolithic than it has been presented (and certainly more civic-minded) and as an entity that was defeated on occasion, but still incredibly powerful. Historian William Deverell writes:

"Although the Southern Pacific Railroad did not control events and individuals to the degree that older and newer commentaries have charged, it *was* an extremely powerful entity nonetheless."[83]

Opposition to the Southern Pacific formed from other business groups, who argued that the overarching domination stagnated the state's economic position. Leaders of the reform movement founded the Lincoln-Roosevelt League in Los Angeles in 1907.[84] The conviction for corruption of San Francisco boss Abraham Ruef[85] was a significant victory, but the reformers were still stymied.[86] "The Lincoln-Roosevelt League would remain but a potentially dangerous irritant to the Southern Pacific machine unless it could place its own candidate in the governor's chair."[87]

The progressives finally had their opening in 1910. In 1906, Democrat Theodore Bell ran a strong race focused on the Southern Pacific, but he still lost to Republican James Gillet..[88] For

---

[80] In an attempt to stave off the recall, Harper resigned before the vote. This gambit failed, as the court held that the recall would go forward against his successor. Bird and Ryan, *The Recall of Public Officers*, 239-240.In 2003, some commentators discussed a similar proposal to prevent the Gray Davis recall, with Davis resigning and Lieutenant Governor Cruz Bustamante taking over and preempting the recall. Nothing came of this plan. Harley Sorensen, "How Davis Could Stop the Recall Madness," *San Francisco Chronicle* (July 28, 2003).

[81] Frank Norris, The Octopus: A Story of California. See William Deverell, Railroad Crossing: Californians and the Railroad, *1850-1910* (Berkeley: University of California Press, 1994), for an in-depth examination of this school of history and the impact of *The Octopus* on reformers as well as latter-day historians.

[82] George Mowry, The California Progressives (Berkeley: University of California Press, 1951), 9.

[83] Deverell, *Railroad Crossing,* 41. Sitton, *John Randolph Haynes,* 86. Also see Richard Orsi, Sunset Limited: The Southern Pacific Railroad and the Development of the American West 1850-1930, University of California Press, 2007.

[84] Haynes, originally wary of the League's chances of success, preferred to focus his attention on the Direct Legislation League. His view changed with the League's successes. Sitton, *John Randolph Haynes,* 90.

[85] Franklin Hichborn felt that the Ruef prosecution was critical to the Progressives' later success, though the prosecution failed in the prosecution of others. "Had there been no San Francisco graft prosecution, there would in 1910, have been no successful political uprising in California." Franklin Hichborn, "The System" as uncovered by the San Francisco Graft Prosecution, (San Francisco: Press of James H. Barry, 1915), 464.

[86] See Franklin Hichborn, The Story of the California Legislature 1909. (San Francisco: Press of the James H. Berry Company, 1909) for a story of the Espee's chief political lobbyist stopping passage of the initiative with one phone call.

[87] Spencer Olin, California's Prodigal Sons (Berkeley: University of California Press, 1968), 20.

[88] *Fresno Republican (*Oct. 31, 1906), as quoted in Mowry, 62.

1910, the reformers convinced the second Boss Reuf prosecutor Hiram Johnson to run for the Republican nomination.[89] Johnson was a reluctant standard bearer,[90] but the choice was inspired. He became a single issue candidate. The slogan: "kick the Southern Pacific out of politics." Johnson was helped by the use of a new California law – the direct primary. He defeated four other contenders, and then faced off against Bell, once again the Democratic nominee. "Johnson was conducting a more flamboyant campaign than Bell and had a more disciplined party apparatus, thoroughly under the control of the Lincoln-Roosevelt League."[91] Johnson was not shy about accusing Bell of accepting the support of the Southern Pacific.[92] Whether that helped, or whether the strong Republican lean of California made the difference, Johnson triumphed, 177,000 to 155,000.

The next session of the legislature proved to be one of the most important in California history. Journalist Franklin Hichborn, who wrote the most important contemporary works on the progressive revolution, stated: "There was to be no Republican policies nor Democratic policies, only administration policies."[93] Hiram Johnson's inaugural speech showed where the priorities may lie: "How best can we arm the people to protect themselves hereafter?"[94]

The legislature quickly adopted provision for ballot measures to approve the initiative and referendum. The recall, however, ran into some trouble.

California and the recall of judges controversy

There was no area that saw more debate than the discussion of whether judges should be subject to the recall. For progressives, there was no question: "As for the state judiciary, it was the considered opinion of Dr. John R. Haynes that the Southern Pacific's domination of no other arm of government was as complete or pernicious."[95]

The argument fit right into the general progressive philosophy of devolving power to the people. Governor Johnson said that: "Under an elective system the Recall should be applied to all officers. It will make no judge weaker, nor a strong judge less strong. It will be a warning and a menace to the corrupt only."[96]

However, with the doctrine of judicial independence a powerful counterargument, the recall of judges became the best target of attack. Hichborn noted "no sooner had the administration taken

---

[9] Johnson took over the graft trials after the first prosecutor, Francis Heney, was shot in the head and wounded. Heney was also discussed, and rejected, as a possible candidate for governor. He later became a bitter enemy of Johnson.

[] Michael A. Weathers and Hal Bochin, Hiram Johnson: Political Revivalist (Latham, MD.: University Press of America, 1995), 22.

[] Kevin Starr, Inventing the Dream (New York: Oxford University Press, 1985), 253.

[] Olin, Prodigal Sons, 31. Bell was backed by the Southern Pacific as "the lesser of two reform evils." Sitton, John Randolph Haynes, 91.

[] Franklin Hichborn, The Story of the California Legislature of 1911 (San Francisco: Press of the James H. Berry Company, 1911), 47

[] Inaugural Address of Governor Hiram Johnson. January 3, 1911. Hichborn, 1911, iv.

[] Mowry, California Progressives ,14. The state Supreme Court had decided fifty-seven of seventy-nine cases in the company's favor from 1895 to 1910. Olin, Prodigal Sons, 3.

[] Hichborn, 1911, 138.

up recall legislation, then strong opposition to the recall of the Judiciary developed in the ranks of the progressives themselves." The fight crossed partisan lines, with Charles Wheeler, a leading progressive Republican, saying that the recall of the judiciary "strike at the very foundation of the government in which I live...."[97]

The drafters of the proposed legislation, the Republican State Central Committee's Committee on Direct Legislation, left the recall of judges out of the original draft.[98] The *Los Angeles Times* said, "the sentiment here is strongly against going to that extreme (the inclusion of the recall of judges)...."[99]

The legislature did not leave it out, leading to an "oratorical duel" between Wheeler and progressive hero, Senator Francis Heney. Wheeler argued that the recall of judges "will mean the last of the republic of our fathers when you pass this bill, for we will pass from a constitutional democracy built by them, to a pure democracy and all its dangers."[100] Heney's speech received the full treatment in the *Los Angeles Times*, with the headline: "Heney Violently Assails the United State Constitution." The LAT quotes Heney as arguing that: "The right of the Supreme Court to pass on the constitutionality of the acts of Congress was a stolen right."[101] The U.S. Supreme Court's controversial decision repealing the income tax[102] loomed large in any debate of the Progressive Era. That decision, and others, led the progressives to believe that the courts were the tool of moneyed interests. Wheeler acknowledged the income tax decision but argued that there were other methods to remove judges.[103]

The recall of judges provision was in danger of being removed, with even Johnson expressing "grave doubts" to Haynes that it would be approved.[104] But the California Supreme Court's own actions managed to save the day for the recall.
The court granted a rehearing of prison sentences in the San Francisco graft trials, with four members signing on. One of the members, Justice Henshaw, who was seen as close to the Southern Pacific, was roasted for signing the order and going on vacation "without considering the briefs which had been filed in the case."[105] The uproar changed the dynamic. Impeachment charges against the justices were now considered,[106] and the recall started moving forward again. "[Assemblyman] John C. March, Sacramento, declared that until the last ten days he was against the recall of the judiciary, but the events of the last two weeks have changed his mind...."[107]. In the Senate and the Assembly combined, the vote was 106-14. Hichborn cited the vote for the recall as "unique."

Every member of both houses voted for or against it. Seldom, if ever, has the entire vote of the

---

[97]Ibid, 102-103.
[98]Ibid, 103.
[99]*Los Angeles Times* (February 4, 1911).
[100]Ibid.
[101]*Los Angeles Times* (February 5, 1911).
[102] *Pollock v. Farmers' Loan and Trust Company,* 157 U.S. 429
[103]*Los Angeles Times* (February 4, 1911).
[104]Bird and Ryan, *Recall of Public Officers,* 49.
[105] Hichborn, *1911,* 112. See also Mowry, *California Progressives,*142.
[106]*Los Angeles Times* (February 16, 1911).
[107] *Sacramento Bee* (March 7, 1911).

California legislature been cast for a measure... Never before, probably, had a measure before the California legislature been so thoroughly argued and discussed.[108]

The legislature's approval was step one. The people still had to approve the ballot measures. The *Los Angeles Times* helped lead the charge against the new laws, referring to direct democracy as "freak legislation."[109] According to the *Times*, the passage of the recall "show[ed the] remarkable caprice of ballot wielders."[110] Despite its hatred for direct democracy and the progressives, the newspaper was itself a leading opponent of the Southern Pacific.[111]

In October 1911, the people went to the ballot box to consider twenty-three amendments on the ballot, including women's suffrage and all three direct democracy provisions.[112] Twenty-two of the amendments passed,[113] with the recall garnering the most votes and the second largest margin,[114] with 76.82% in favor of the recall, 178,115-53,755.

In the next several years, the recall got a workout. However, Haynes felt that "the only fault that can be charged against it (direct legislation) is a somewhat excessive conservatism."[115]

Center Stage: How the Recall Against Judges Shaped the 1912 Presidential Election

The 1912 Presidential election, at the zenith of the Progressive movement, is not the most important election in US history but it is arguably the most exciting.[116] The Republicans were split between progressives and conservatives, and one of the issues that brought about the division was the recall – with President William Howard Taft and his predecessor and erstwhile friend, former President Theodore Roosevelt, on opposite sides.

Continuing the battling motif, as opposed to California Governor Hiram Johnson's "gun behind the door," Taft saw the recall as the "'hair trigger' form of government."[117] Taft jumped into the

---

[108]Hichborn, *1911*, 137.

[109]*Los Angeles Times* (October 10, 1911).

[110]*Los Angeles Times* (October 11, 1911).

[111]Olin, *Prodigal Sons*, 5.

[112]"Triple Freak of Initiative, Referendum and Recall certainly carried." *Los Angeles Times* (October 11, 1911).

[113] The one that failed allowed transportation companies to give free or discounted passes to public officials. Check out Sam Rayburn rejecting free railroad passes for a look at how this issue played elsewhere. Robert Caro, The Path to Power: The Years of Lyndon Johnson, Vintage Books, 1982. 310

[114] Proposition 15 got 79.27% of the vote (168,010-43,943). Ballotpedia notes that Prop. 15 changed the minimum timeframe for the use of textbooks in public schools to four years. https://ballotpedia.org/California_Period_of_Use_of_Textbooks,_Proposition_15_(October_1911)

[115]Haynes, *Direct Government*, 9.

[116] Think about it – the only time three presidents faced off against each other; Roosevelt shot before giving a speech; the first real presidential primary race; the only time the 2/3rds rule blocked a candidate in the Democratic convention; the last sitting Vice President to die in office; a fourth party candidate garnering 6 percent of the vote; and historical heavy hitters like Robert La Follete, William Jennings Bryan, Champ Clark, Silent Charlie Murphy and Eugene Debs are the second tier names. There are elections with much bigger issues at play, but for pure excitement, 1912 beats them all.

[117]William Howard Taft, Popular Government: Its Essence, Its Permanence and Its Perils,(New Haven: Yale Univ. Press, 1913) 81.

fight full force on August 15, 1911, with his vetoing of the Arizona Constitution over its recall of judges' provision. Taft called the recall "legalized terrorism."[118]

While he saved his most vituperative comments for the recall of judges, he despised the entire endeavor. The recall would turn officials into "mere puppets in office who can not enter upon proper public policies ... because they feel that their purpose will be misunderstood."

The recall is nothing but the logical outcome of the proposition ... that government must follow the course of popular passion and momentary expression of the people without deliberation and without opportunity for full information.[119]

Progressives were outraged, with some claiming that he was vetoing "the basic principles of popular government." According to historian of the Progressive Movement, George Mowry: "...his veto of the statehood bill had further convinced the progressive forces that at heart he was a hopeless conservative." [120] (The veto worked only as a statement. Arizona removed the provision and, after the state was admitted, promptly put it back in the Constitution.)

Standing directly in the path was the still incredibly popular Roosevelt, who said in defense of direct democracy: "I have heard no argument advanced against the proposition, save that it will make the public officer timid and always currying favor with the mob. That argument means that you can fool all the people all the time, and is an avowal of disbelief of democracy."[121]

As with many Progressives at the time, the courts drew Roosevelt's ire for their stridently pro-business stands. Among the ideas that he backed was a push for the recall of state judicial decisions,[122] an action that horrified conservatives. Taft compared it to "the French Revolution or in that bubbling anarchy that once characterized the South American Republics."[123]

In his formal announcement of candidacy, Roosevelt mentioned that the recall of the judiciary could be used as a last resort. As the campaign wore on and got more bitter, and Roosevelt took on more of the progressive mantle, he still hedged on the recall of judges. He cited his own state of New York as one that did not need a recall for judges. However, Roosevelt claimed, "democracy has a right to approach the sanctuary of the courts when a special interest has corruptly found sanctuary there."[124]

Many of Roosevelt's close supporters, notably Roosevelt's Secretary of State and Secretary of

---

[118] Special Message of the President of the United States Returning Without Approval House Joint Resolution No. 14. 8 https://www.archives.gov/legislative/features/nm-az-statehood/taft-veto.html
[119] Taft. 83-85.
[120] Theodore Roosevelt and the Progressive Movement, 171-172.
[121] Theodore Roosevelt. The Right of the People to Rule. delivered in Carnegie Hall, March 20, 1912. Senate Document no. 473. 62nd Congress, 2nd Session. 4
[122] This recall would allow a "popular curb" on the judicial power to declare acts unconstitutional. It has since nearly disappeared from the literature, and it was not mentioned by either of the two most recent books on the recall Edward Hartnett, "Why is the Supreme Court of the United States Protecting State Judges from Popular Democracy?" Texas Law Review, 75. Tex. L. Rev. 907, 935
[123] Mowry, 215-16.
[124] Roosevelt. The Right of the People to Rule. 5.

War Elihu Root, and his own son-in-law Nicholas Longworth, backed Taft, and the recall, specifically against judges and judicial decisions, may have been a big reason why. The race was an exciting one and Roosevelt managed to win nine of the last 10 states. However, Taft still triumphed, in what was the first presidential primary campaign, thanks to the support of these former Roosevelt supporters (and, in part on a Southern Strategy[125] where he didn't need to actually win votes).

Mowry notes: "He might have won over a great portion of conservative Republicans if he had not also included his plan for the democratization of the judiciary, his scheme, however for the recall of state judicial decisions alienated most that element."[126]

The primary split the party, with Roosevelt marching out to form the Progressive Party (also popularly known as the Bull Moose Party). Never the most energetic man, Taft seemed to accept his eventual loss in the general election and ran a very 19th century style campaign with little travel or actual in-person campaigning. The split guaranteed the election of New Jersey Governor Woodrow Wilson. While Wilson shared many of the Progressive goals, he quietly put direct democracy in the background if he did not drop it altogether.[127] The outbreak of World War I had a limiting effect on any progressive legislative goals, which certainly prevented recalls from becoming a major issue during the rest of his term.

Future Supreme Court Chief Justice Taft did not let the issue drop. One of his action items upon leaving the presidency was to write a book attacking the Direct Legislation movements entitled Popular Government: Its Essence, Its Permanence and Its Perils, where he tarred the ideas with the labels of socialistic and anarchistic. Taft, who questioned the entire basis for the democratization of the judiciary,[128] was joined in his opposition by the American Bar Association (ABA), which set up the Committee to Oppose the Judicial Recall. The committee monitored the status of debates on the judicial recall and sponsored counter recall activity throughout the country. The highly politicized nature of the debate can be seen in the attacks by the ABA's committee on the proponents of the recall. They are referred to individually as socialist agitators who denounce "our constitution and our entire system of government as unworthy of the respect or regard of the citizen."[129]

As we will see in the California and Wisconsin adoption debates, the recall of judges was seen as the best method of attack on the recall, with conservatives seeing it as a worthy subject of attack as late as 1926. However, the separate topic of the recall of judicial decisions that was pushed by

---

[125] Joshua Spivak, "Biden's Southern Strategy: How the Red States Could Still Win Him the Nomination," *Newsweek*, October 24, 2019. https://www.newsweek.com/biden-southern-strategy-primaries-red-states-nomination-1467562

[126] Hartnett, 937. Also quoting Mowry, 138.

[127] "Opposes the Judicary Recall," Merced County Sun, January 19, 1912. At this fairly late date, Wilson is seen as finally coming around to the initiative and referendum. However, he said "Regarding judiciary recall, I can say that I do not favor it, as it attacks a symptom instead of a disease." Also, Hartnett, 955. "Wilson, unlike Roosevelt, but like Root, Taft, and tha American Bar Association, was a firm supporter of judicial independence..."

[128] Ibid. 169-170. ...judicial branch is not representative of a majority of the people... They are not popular epresentatives. On the contrary, to fill their office properly, they must be independent.

[129] Report of the Committee to Oppose the Judicial Recall. Presented at the meeting of the American Bar association, October 22-24, 1914.. 7-8.

Roosevelt dropped off the map soon after the 1912 election. According to Bird and Ryan, after the Supreme Court of Colorado declared it void in 1921, it disappeared as a topic of debate. In actual practice, the recall of judges never met the fears of Taft and conservatives.[130] There have been only a handful of judges who faced a recall in U.S. history[131] and six states have a specific carve out, exempting judges from the recall. In 2017, the Nevada Supreme Court threw out the portion of the recall law targeting judges (under what I'd consider astonishingly terrible logic, which we'll get to soon). In 1913, San Francisco Police Court Justice Charles Weller was ousted in a very close vote (30,784-29,934) over complaints that he set low bail for rape (and notably, statutory rape) defendants, allowing them to skip town.[132] In 1924, a Superior Court Judge in Arizona, Stephen H. Abbey was kicked out in a recall, leading to a notable court case.[133] In 1932, Los Angeles Superior Court Judges John L. Fleming, Dailey S. Stafford and Walter Guerin were kicked out in a recall. In 1977, Wisconsin Judge Archie Simonson was ousted in a recall and in 1982 Wisconsin Judge William Reinecke survived one – both of these were about disparaging comments made from the bench about sexual assault victims. These were the last recall of a judge until 2018.

The most famous "recalls" of judges in US history were not really recalls. There were five attempts to recall California Supreme Court Chief Justice Rose Bird over the court's liberal stance on issues, none of which got enough signatures to get on the ballot. Eventually, Bird and Justices Cruz Reynoso and Joseph Grodin were kicked out of office in a mandatory replacement race that is sometimes mistaken for a recall.[134] Likewise, three Iowa Supreme Court judges in 2010 lost their office in retention races for their votes on legalizing same-sex marriage, but these were not recall despite news coverage to the contrary.[135]

In 2018, California Superior Court Judge Aaron Persky was ousted in a recall vote over complaints about a lenient sentence for a Stanford swimmer convicted of rape. This recall drew national attention (as may have the Wisconsin ones), though so far it is not clear if there will be any impact beyond the one vote. Notably, a number of these recalls of judges are focused on leniency in sex crimes. There were judges targeted in Orange County, California and Montana over the same subject.

---

[130] As mentioned above, Patrick Buchanan tried to revive the idea for his 1996 presidential campaign, but that went nowhere.
[131] In addition to the ones I've seen, there are local positions with a title of judge, but are more of an executive/legislative position, so that doesn't count.
[132] Bird & Ryan. Also Estelle B. Freedman, "When Feminists Take on Judges Over Rape," New York Times, June 10, 2016.
[133] Abbey v. Green, 28 Ariz. 53 (Sup. Ct. 1925) https://casetext.com/case/abbey-v-green . John D. Leshy, The Arizona State Constitution, Oxford University Press, 2013. Leshy notes that this is the only recall of a judge in state's history. 248-249
[134] "Rose Bird" California Journal, November 1, 1999. Bird, Justices Joseph Grodin and Cruz Reynoso were voted out of office in a mandatory retention election, a separate provision in the California Constitution. It is widely, though erroneously, believed that Bird was recalled. See John Balzar, "Few Rules to Go By: Justice Bird's Recall Becoming Epic Battle," Los Angeles Times (April 7, 1985) and the subsequent correction on April 10, 1985 for an example of this error.
[135] A.G. Sulzberger, "Ouster of Iowa Judges Sends Signal to Bench," New York Times, November 3, 2010. "Leaders of the recall campaign said the results should be a warning to judges elsewhere." https://www.nytimes.com/2010/11/04/us/politics/04judges.html

In 1912, the recall of judges impacted United States history, helping to give a temporary break in the Republican domination of federal politics from the onset of McKinleynomics to the Great Depression. We could claim that it may have greatly impacted world politics, namely if Taft or Roosevelt were president, we would have had a different response to World War I. But in terms of actual impact on the judiciary, it remains a minor footnote.

Wisconsin: How Progressives' Houdini Act Brought the Recall Back from the Dead

When you think of the states that are the big users of the recall, Wisconsin stands out for two reasons. 1. It is the only one of those states not to also possess the ballot initiative. 2. It was a relatively late adopter. This leads to a basic question – why was Wisconsin's adoption of the recall different from other states?

Unlike California, the history of Wisconsin's adoption of the recall has been effectively buried. I read through most of the 1926 issues of both the Milwaukee Sentinel and Milwaukee Journal (at the time, separate papers) and found very little of substance that would explain why Wisconsin passed the recall in 1926.[136] Neither *Wisconsin Magazine of History* nor the History of Wisconsin Volume V by Paul Glad have any discussion about the adoption of the recall.

However, during the Governor Scott Walker recall, we finally had some light shed on the issue. Christian Schneider, who was a fellow at the Wisconsin Policy Research Institute, published an extremely useful piece that provides critical insight into the adoption of the recall.[137] I concur in part and dissent in part with his conclusions, but this is really the one piece worth checking out. 1926 is not where we start. Instead, we have to go back to Wisconsin's Progressive salad years, from 1901-1914. In this case, we do have a book that's useful, The History of Wisconsin Volume IV by John Buenker.[138]

1910-1914 is when most of the early states adopted the recall. Wisconsin, by all reason, should have been among them. The Progressives, under the leadership of Senator Robert La Follette were entrenched in power for more than a decade. They finally made their attempt to adopt direct democracy starting in 1910, which was a banner election year for progressives' nation-wide, as the Democrats captured the House, their first time in control of either house since 1894.[139] In the Wisconsin 1910 legislative session, the legislature approved the Direct Democracy provisions. The initiative and the referendum sailed through, but the recall hit a bump. Just like

---

[136] I did find a great article about Harry Houdini – he died right when the election was about to be held. I turned that into an article for the Forward. Joshua Spivak, The True Story of Harry Houdini's Tefillin," *The Forward*, March 4, 2015. http://forward.com/articles/214053/the-true-story-of-harry-houdinis-tefillin/#idc-cover

[137] Christian Schneider, "The History of the Recall in Wisconsin," *WPRI Report*, Volume 25, No. 3 April 2012. WPRI is a "free market think tank" on the right and clearly opposed the Walker recall. In the piece and in others he wrote, Schneider has an obvious political point of view (which is fine – many of these pieces do, they are just so far in the past that we overlook it), but make no mistake about it, he's got the goods. http://www.wpri.org/Reports/Volume25/Vol25No3/Vol25No3.html

[138] John Buenker, The History of Wisconsin Vol. IV: The Progressive Era 1893-1914, Wisconsin Historical Society Press, 1998. Unfortunately, I did not take notes on this book.

[139] The Democrats had lost the Senate in 1894 as well and had been completely shut out in Washington since 1896. The Democrats did get a measure of power earlier in 1910 during a revolt between Speaker Joe Cannon and George Norris.

in California, the proposal to adopt a recall against judges proved a hurdle. But it was only a temporary one. The legislature still easily approved the entire recall provision (which was substantively somewhat different than Wisconsin's current law – you can read Schneider's article for those details. The most important changes appear to be a one-year grace period and the change from a registered voter signature requirement, rather than the much looser eligible voter one from 1926).

If it was in another state, it may have sailed through right then. But Wisconsin's law on ballot propositions is different from many states. They have to be passed by two separate legislative sessions. So instead of 1912, another great year for progressives, it got on the ballot in 1914. By the time it got to the ballot, the backlash against progressives in Wisconsin had begun. The progressives failed to unite on a Republican primary candidate and split their vote (the state was Republican dominated, so the primary was the big vote). Due to the removal of the Mary Ann[140] ranked choice or instant run-off provision[141] (a favorite of La Follette), the conservative was victorious in the gubernatorial race (though the progressives won the Senate primary). Furthermore, on the national level, there was the expected mid-term backlash. President Woodrow Wilson's supporters got drubbed.[142]

The result was that all 10 ballot proposals that would reshape the state, including the initiative, referendum and recall, went down in flames. None of the 10 proposals got 40% of the vote. The initiative was apparently finished. But the recall went on to live another day.

The progressives came back to power in 1922. And here is where we get lost. The legislature passed the recall in that session and then again in the 1924-26 session. 1924 was a good year for conservative Republicans nationwide.[143] However, it was a great year for progressives in Wisconsin. Robert La Follette ran for president and won the state (and 4.8 million votes nationwide). His race undoubtedly helped the party keep the state progressive for the 1924 session.

I didn't see much about the adoption of the recall (though perhaps I have to look through 1923, 1924 and 1925 to find coverage). The death of La Follette in June 1925 may have given the

---

[140] Not sure why it is called the Mary Ann, though I 'm guessing that was what you called the second choice date in those days. Could be wrong. I do love the old time names for election laws – check out Robert Caro's The Powerbroker for a discussion of the term "Ripper Bill" and how the fact that Robert Moses knew the term showed how you should fear him.

[141] I can't even find a link on google to share on the Mary Ann provision, but it is a form of ranked choice. There is book/play by L.T. Crabtree, "The Wayback Club: A Text Book on Progressiveism in Wisconsin" on Google Book· that you can see – though it looks like L.T. may be the publisher. Also, "Fail to Eliminate Dahl's Opponents; Hope in Mary Ann," The Janesville Daily Gazette, August 18, 1914.

[142] The Republicans won 62 seats, though not enough to take control of the House. The nascent Progressives were nearly wiped out – though the machinations regarding the 1916 race is what finally did them in.

[143] 1924 has been overlooked in history, but a pretty critical year in the US. The disastrous Immigration Act had massive repercussions. Notably, the same year, the Democrats ran arguably their most conservative candidate ever for president (opening the way for the La Follette race). Plus, we had the 103rd Ballot and the growth of the KKK. I look at it here in CNBC: https://www.cnbc.com/2016/03/23/the-gop-convention-is-going-to-be-a-hot-mess-commentary.html On the plus side? I guess a hell of a Word Series, with the Big Train, Walter Johnson, getting h only title and the Giants once again victimized by a freak play.

ecall some further push, but there was little discussion of the recall[144] until the end of 1926, where a few critical articles appeared in both the Journal and Sentinel and complaints from the tate bar about a negative impact on judges.

he vote itself was held in November. The recall was not the big ballot initiative that year – that ame day Wisconsin had a vote on whether to allow the sale of beer in defiance of prohibition. No surprise, the Beer Bill passed easily). For the recall, the earliest coverage suggested it going own to defeat. And the end result was a close vote. It only got 50.6% of the vote. Fortunately or recall backers, 1926 was also a good backlash year against Coolidge – the Democrats did ell, and presumably so did progressives.

According to Christian Schneider, the recall law had a very limited focus. It was not about overnors or legislators, but about judges. Here is where we part company.

chneider argues that the debate surrounding the recall appears to be completely about judges, which leads him to the (logical) position that the recall might have been about the removal of idges. From what I saw, he is correct that the focus of the anti-recall forces was certainly on its otential impact on judges. But a look at other states and the national recall battles in the past -- omething that, in his defense, Schneider would not have seen – shows that this is not a surprise.

he recall of judges (and judicial decisions) was clearly the most controversial part of the recall, opposed by even some of the ardent supporters of the recall. It is no surprise, both from a neoretical and a tactical level, that it would be the key focus of negative campaigning. It was the reak point of the recall, and opponents went after it with fervor. Therefore, I would not read uch into the focus on the judiciary. It is more likely that the recall of judges was simply an easy lectoral tactic and probably not an indication of why the recall was adopted. There did not seem o be a judicial decision that precipitated the recall discussion (as opposed to in California).

he second point Schneider makes is that at the time, governors only served two-year terms. enators served four, and (like today) Assembly members served two. The law was changed in 967 to give governors a four-year term. Schneider argues that with the "no recalls in the first ear of office" limit, governors would not have really been a target. Again, I disagree.

y 1926, Wisconsin had the ability to see numerous recall campaigns, including those against a overnor (North Dakota), three state legislators (California), the mayors of LA, Seattle, Denver id Atlanta. They knew what they were getting into, and they knew how the recall operated.

ote that North Dakota's gubernatorial recall of 1921, the most famous recall in the country, ook place against an official who was elected to a two-year term. The governors of a full half of ie states that had a recall (Arizona, Colorado, Kansas, Michigan and North Dakota) had a two-ear term at that time.[145] It is true that no other states has such a long grace period at the outset of ie term-- California had a 3 month grace period and North Dakota bans a recall if there will be a ce for the position within the year -- but that doesn't prove much. There is a lot of variety in

---

Schneider, "With all this action at the top of the ticket, the recall amendment went virtually unnoticed by the olic or the media until just days before the election."

New Hampshire and Vermont are the only two states that still have a two-year term for Governor.

recall laws, and the reason for the variety is frequently unknown. Legislative bodies rarely consider the recall when drafting election laws, resulting in strange and barely considered problems. I'm not sure why the law was written with a one-year delay, but it would be a great stretch to say that it effectively exempts most major offices in the state.

Schneider also notes that the recalls in Wisconsin in 2011 and 2012 have all been against senators, elected to four-year terms, and none have been launched against current Assembly members, elected to two-year terms. I don't think this proves much. The Senate was targeted because winning three Senate seats would give the Democrats control over the chamber. The Republicans had an enormous majority in the Assembly. If instead it was separated by a few seats, we may have seen Assembly members facing the recall.

Chapter 3: The Use of the Recall on the State Level -- When It's Not In Action, It's In Traction:

In this chapter, we will look at all of the recalls that have taken place on the state level. Before we get to this, let's take a brief look at the popular question of whether a federal official can be recalled.

Federal Recalls:

The recall is constantly brought up for federal officers – sometimes presidents, frequently Senators or Representatives and occasionally even federal judges. Is a recall of a federal official allowable?

The laws in nine states specifically allow for the recall to be used against senators and representatives. And there have been many attempts. A recall effort against Wisconsin Senator Joe McCarthy got 335,000 signatures (they would have needed 403,000). Arkansas, which does not even have a state recall law, also saw an attempted recall of US Senator William J. Fulbright in 1968 by one of his defeated opponents. That effort focused on getting a constitutional amendment on the ballot that would also include federal officials. The petitioners got 57,111 signatures in six weeks; just 4500 short of what they had hoped would work.[146] Senator Frank Church from Idaho was targeted in 1967 over his opposition to the Vietnam War.[147]

In more recent vintage, we've seen recall efforts against Senators Russell Feingold (D-WI), John McCain (R-AZ), Kent Conrad (D-ND), Mary Landrieu (D-LA) and Robert Mendez (D-NJ), as well as Representative Liz Cheney (R-WY). There were also threats of Utah adopting a recall law to attack Senator Mitt Romney (R-UT) after his support for the impeachment. It's worth noting that almost all of these recent recall efforts – even against Republicans – have been pushed by more conservative right wingers.

Despite these attempts, the efforts appeared doomed to failure. The Church recall attempt was thrown out by a district court. The Menendez recall actually survived a state Appellate Court ruling but was stopped in a 2010 New Jersey State Supreme Court decision, which ruled (4-2) that no federal officials are subject to a recall. I was actually quite surprised that two judges voted to allow the recall. North Dakota's Supreme Court also rejected the Conrad recall attempt in the same year. While New Jersey's ruling only operates in that state, there are good reasons to assume that the federal courts would hold the same way.

The overwhelming problem with the recall for federal officials is the U.S. Supreme Court is very unlikely to allow it to move forward. The 1995 Supreme Court's decision striking down term limits for federal officials shows the challenges. Both the decision and the long dissent from Justice Clarence Thomas mention that federal officials are not subject to the recall. Thomas' position – one that would have allowed term limits to be set and also would have allowed for

---

[146]"Fulbright Recalls fails in Arkansas," *New York Times,* July 4, 1970. ttps://www.nytimes.com/1970/07/04/archives/fulbright-recall-fails-in-arkansas.html
[147] Wallace Turner, "Recall Moves Against Opens AA Right Wing Drive to Punish Critics of Vietnam War," *New York Times*, May 25, 1967. https://timesmachine.nytimes.com/timesmachine/1967/05/25/issue.html

some leeway in dealing with elected officials -- notes in referring to a form of punitive instruction that "…such a power would approximate a power of recall, which the Framers denied to the States when they specified the terms of Members of Congress. The Framers may well have thought that state power over salary, like state power to recall, would be inconsistent with the notation that Congress was a national legislature once it assembled."[148]

There have been occasional discussions on adopting a federal recall. A 1987 poll run by the Twentieth Century Fund found popular support for the extension of the recall to federal officials.[149] In 1996, Representative Peter Hoekstra introduced a package of "Voter's Bill of Rights," which would include recalls for senators and congressmen, and there have been occasional calls to recall U.S. senators.[150] Also in 1996, Republican Presidential Candidate Patrick Buchanan advocated adopting the recall for the federal judiciary.[151] None of these discussions went anywhere and there seems little reason to believe that the recall will be put in place on the federal level.

California's Legislature and the Gray Davis Recall

With its long history of using the recall, it may be no surprise that California is the first state to use the recall on the state level. There have been 179 attempted recalls of state level officials in California history, including 55 against Governors, 2 against Lieutenant Governors, 7 against Attorneys General, 30 against State Senators, 50 against Assembly members and 27 against individual Supreme Court justices. Of these attempts, only 11 have reached the ballot.[152]

We'll consider these 11 recalls chronologically broken up as follows: 1913-1914 recalls, the 1994-1995 recalls and the Governor Gray Davis recall. Although our treatment will be brief, we will address the major questions of what, how and why the recall was launched against the particular individual. Our analysis of the legislative recalls will yield important insights in how recalls work and especially with regard to the 1995 recalls, how California and American politics reached its current stage. This understanding will enable us to make sense of the Newsom recall to which we devote the next chapter.

The Early Recalls: 1913-1914

The first set of recalls took place almost immediately after the recall was allowed on the local level:

---

[148] *U.S. Term Limits vs. Thorton*, 514 1U.S. 779, 890.

[149] Cronin, *Direct Democracy,*5.

[150] H.J. Res. 86, 105th Congress. Another Congressman, Mark Neumann signed a petition to recall Wisconsin's two Democratic Senators over their position on abortion. Julie Cohen, "Mark Neumann, Republican Hothead," *The Economist* (May 3, 1997). In addition, in 1995, California Senatorial candidate Michael Huffington, who spent $30 million of dollars of his own money in a losing Senate bid in 1994, and whose ex-wife Arianna ran for election in the Davis Recall, was set to hold a press conference calling for the recall of Senator Dianne Feinstein, the winning candidate in the election. According to the San Francisco Chronicle, Huffington did not hold the press conference after he "was advised that, by law, a U.S. Senator cannot be recalled" Susan Yoachum "Huffington Plan for a Recall is Recalled," *San Francisco Chronicle* (February 27, 1995).

[151] "Term Limits for Judges," *New Jersey Law Journal* (September 4, 1995).

[152] California Secretary of State website, accessed on August 9, 2021. https://www.sos.ca.gov/elections/recalls/recall-history-california-1913-present

1913: Senator Marshall Black (R) was indicted in 1912 for embezzling funds from the Palo Alto Mutual Building and Loan Association.[153] The Republican County Central Committee launched a successful recall, with the election held on January 2, 1913, where "an unusually small vote was cast."[154]

1913: Senator James Owens (D) faced a recall led by labor groups as a "test of the effectiveness of the recall against an unfaithful legislator who fails to live up to pre-election promises and platform pledges." This was not the first recall Owens had faced, as he had successfully fended off a recall when he served as a Councilman. The recall backfired on labor – instead of showing their strength it was "…conclusive proof that labor planks in a party platform are not always to be taken too seriously...."[155] Senator Owens managed to fight off the recall by the comfortable margin of 6,749 to 5,177.

1914: Senator Edwin E. Grant (D) was one of the more complex recalls against a state-level official. It was 80 years before another one reached the ballot. In 1912, Grant, with the support of Hiram Johnson, defeated incumbent Senator Eddie Wolfe, one of the leaders of the San Francisco conservatives, by ninety-five votes. A recall was started by the San Francisco political machine, according to Grant's backers, due to Grant's opposition to "vice conditions" with his sponsoring of the Redlight Abatement Act.[156] Of course, the act was not cited in the petitions,[157] because, according to Bird and Ryan, "to recall a state senator for having opposed vice conditions did not seem possible even in San Francisco...."[158]

The entire process was clouded with controversy. Twice, the recall petitions failed, once because the signatures burned, the other time because of forged or irregular signatures. The third try succeeded (though it led to a later Senate investigation). The opposition candidate was none other than former Senator Eddie Wolfe. Hichborn claimed "some of those who were circulating petitions against Grant had stated the petition 'was to put Wolfe back in the Senate in place of Grant.'"[159] This aspect of the recall, the reversal of an election verdict, is not discussed in depth in the writings on the Grant election. Grant's supporters argued that the recall would decide whether "forces of vice" would regain control and also cited the cost of the "unnecessary expense" of the recall as a reason to vote for Grant.[160] On October 8, 1914, Grant was removed by a 531 vote margin and Wolfe elected in his place. A little over fifty percent of the district voted in the election. Progressives denounced the vote, but the Los Angeles Times, a committed opponent to the Progressive cause, rejoiced in Grant's defeat and wrongly predicted problems for

---

[153]Black pleaded guilty to the charges and received a 10-year jail sentence.

[154]*Los Angeles Times* (January 3, 1913).

[155]Bird and Ryan, *Recall of Public Officers,* 272-274

[156]The act allowed citizens to sue the owner of a house of prostitution, and close the building as a nuisance. Franklin Hichborn, The Story of the California Legislature 1915 (San Francisco: Press of the James H. Berry Company, 1915), 67. Also see "Senator Grant Faces Recall Poll Thursday," *San Francisco Bulletin* (October 7, 1914).

[157] The focus of the petitions were on three bills: one prohibited the sale of liquor at the Panama-Pacific Exposition (votes in favor of prohibition could be considered an act of political suicide in wet San Francisco); a second, which he opposed, would have prevented most marriages from being solemnized until five days after the issuance of a license; the third, which he also opposed, would have given California authors and publishers preference over those from other states in the preparation and publication of school books.

[158]Bird and Ryan, *Recall of Public Officers,* 276.

[159]Hichborn, *1915*, 78.

[160]"Senator Grant Faces Recall Poll Thursday," *San Francisco Bulletin* (October 7, 1914).

the Progressives and Governor Hiram Johnson in the upcoming election.[161] Grant protested the election based on irregularities in the petitions. Progressives like Hichborn scorned the Senate committee that investigated and dismissed the matter, and argued that the investigation was incomplete.

The recall of Grant and other exercises of direct democracy provisions by opponents of the Progressives brought calls for changes in the procedure. In his message to the legislature, Johnson called for action saying: "It would be idle to deny... that certain abuses have arisen... It is our duty to remedy those abuses...."[162] Without specific guidelines on how to revise the recall, the legislature stumbled to a solution. The first idea was to split the recall and the selection of a new officer into two separate elections. Haynes strenuously objected to this change and claimed that the problems lay in the failure of local officials to enforce the law.[163] Eventually, the legislature settled for a token change of increasing the penalty for forging a name on a petition. The more partisan nature of the state-level recall is explained by one political scientist as the reason for its lack of use: "Signing a petition for recall is often more than repudiating a single state official - it is also a rejection of his or her party." [164]

Legislative Recall Battles of 1994-1995

After a nearly eighty-year absence from state-level political battles, the recall came back with a vengeance during the legislative sessions of 1994-95. Three assembly members and one senator faced recall elections in this period and two were removed. The surge of recalls was in part due to the historic election results of 1994. For the first time since 1954, the Republican Party managed to capture control of both houses of the United States Congress. The party also won a majority of the gubernatorial elections throughout the country. In California, in addition to re-electing Pete Wilson as governor, the Republican Party had managed to obtain a majority in the Assembly. The parliamentary maneuvering that ruled the new Assembly led to the recall gaining an important role in the political process.

1994: Senate President Pro Tempore David Roberti was finishing up his last term in the Senate and was running for state Treasurer. Roberti was a leader in passing a ban on semiautomatic assault weapons in 1989, which led anti-gun control forces to try and make him a test case, one that drew national attention as a test of the strength of the gun lobby. [165] Even with only twenty-five percent turnout, Roberti easily defeated the recall on April 12, 1994, garnering fifty-nine

---

[161] "Grant Recall a Sensation. Was a Democratic Tool of Gov. Johnson," *Los Angeles Times* (October 10, 1914). The article describes the recall as an "absolute repudiation of Gov. Johnson's administration." Johnson was re-elected later that year.
[162] Governor Johnson's biennial message to the 1915 Legislature as quoted in Hichborn, *1915*, 102.
[163] Ibid, 101-102.
[164] Sych, 9.
[165] The recall proponents attempted to use other issues, such as corruption and voter anger in the campaign, but newspaper accounts focused on the gun-control issue. See William Hamilton, "Gun Control Stance Makes California Legislator Target of Recall" *Washington Post* (April 10, 1994). "NRA Endorsed bid to recall gun-contr advocate Roberti" *Associated Press* (April 1, 1994).

percent of the vote. [166]

Roberti and other commentators said that the recall did cost him in his race for Treasurer, as he had to spend $800,000 to keep his position[167] and took time away from campaigning.[168] However, other observers had a different view, as Roberti was thought to be a "tired commodity," in the Treasurer race, running against a deep-pocketed candidate who won the support of both of California's U.S. Senators.[169] According to this view, the recall gave his campaign new life.

A National Rifle Association lobbyist argued that the recall attempt had helped weaken support for gun control bills,[170] though that is debatable. It may have simply served as a visible precursor to the gun lobby's success nationwide in 1994.

There were two postscripts to this recall. First, in November, California voters approved a proposition slightly revising the recall law.[171] Second, the organization that waged the campaign against Roberti, Californians Against Corruption, was charged with hiding the sources of donations received, and was fined by the State Fair Political Practices Commission a record-breaking $800,000 for the violations.[172]

1995: The Year the Recall Broke: The "mania for recall elections,"[173] as the *California Journal* put it, began with a political earthquake: the election of 1994. The Republican Party scored across-the-board victories and succeeded in gaining a razor-thin forty-one to thirty-nine seat majority in the California Assembly, their first majority in twenty-five years. The Republicans expected to be able to elect their own leader as speaker, an enormously powerful position in the Assembly.[174] They would finally be able to topple their Democratic nemesis, Speaker Willie Brown, who had served in that position for the previous fourteen years. The Democrats were focused on stopping Jim Brulte, the Republican leader, whom they considered an extremely effective leader, from gaining the speakership.[175] However, due to the casting of one Republican vote for the Democratic candidate for speaker, which led to "[g]asps heard throughout the

---

[66] Lisa M. Krieger, "Gun Lobby draws bead on Roberti for recall; State Senator's foes organize to make him an example because of his assault-weapon bills," *San Francisco Examiner* (March 27, 1994). "Roberti Slays NRA dragon," *California Journal* (May 1, 1994).
[67]"Treaurer" *California Journal Weekly* (November 21, 1994).
[68]*Orange County Register* (June 9, 1994).
[69] Edward Epstein, "Recall Victory Gives Roberti an Edge in Treasurer's Race" *San Francisco Chronicle* (April 14, 994). Also "Roberti slays NRA dragon" *California Journal* (May 1, 1994).
[70]*Fresno Bee* (June 25, 1994).
[1] The change allowed recalls to be delayed and combined with a regularly scheduled election if the recall was scheduled to take place within 180 days of the election. "Senate Tries to Amend Recalls," *San Francisco Examiner* (May 10, 1994).
[2]"C.A. Upholds $1.1 Million Fine on Roberti Antagonists, Largest Penalty Ever Imposed Under Reform Act," *Metropolitan News Enterprise* (May 30, 2003). With interest, the penalty has increased to $1.1 million. *California Journal Weekly* (December 18, 1995).
Jon Matthews, "Republican says he'll seize Assembly post from Brown," *Sacramento Bee* (November 11, 1994).
James Richardson, <u>Willie Brown: A Biography</u> (Berkeley: University of California Press, 1996), 373. See also d. According to Richardson, the Democrats were especially concerned that Brulte would be able to consolidate victory and manage to keep the Assembly Republican for years to come.

chamber"[176] the Assembly was tied and eventually, through further political maneuvers,[177] re-elected Willie Brown to the speakership.

Republicans filed several recall attempts, and two made the ballot: Renegade Republican Assemblyman, Paul Horcher, who voted for Brown for Speaker and declared himself an independent; and Assemblyman Michael Machado (D), who promised to be "an independent voice"[178] in the Assembly during his campaign.

The Democrats attempted to portray Horcher as an independent-minded reformer, with little success.[179] He was defeated on May 16, 1995, by a margin of sixty-three to thirty-seven percent. Voter turnout was thirty-three percent. Absentee ballots totaled fifty-three percent of the vote cast, sixty-nine percent of which went against Horcher.[180]

Machado, who held a marginal seat and barely won his election, was targeted under the claim that he "lied to his constituents by telling them he would not vote for Brown."[181] The *San Francisco Chronicle*, in denouncing the attempt, described the rationale for the recall: "he actually voted for the leader of his own party to be speaker of the Assembly."[182] This was a rerun election, as the person who finished first in the replacement was the same person Machado beat in the previous election.[183] Republican Assemblyman Bernie Richter, criticized the recall attempt against Machado as "banana republic," saying: "It was an attack on the validity of the election results."[184] Helped by the fact that Brown had already left the speakership by the time of the recall vote, the voters rejected the recall on August 22, 1995, choosing to retain him 31,209 to 18,068. In his previous election, Machado won by 1,764 votes.[185]

After Horcher was recalled and replaced, though before the Machado recall, Brown once again proved his mastery over the Republicans. In June, in what was referred to as "a stunning farewell

---

[176] The California Assembly has a history of cross-party voting for Speakers. Willie Brown was elected Speaker due to Republican votes, and he used Republican support to ward off a challenge to his rule in 1988. See Richardson, *Willie Brown,* 265-271, 342. For a look at events from Horcher's point of view, and how the Republicans ostracized him in 1992 for taking a position on Ways & Means committee: "Where are they now? Paul Horcher," Capitol Weekly, December 29, 2017. https://capitolweekly.net/where-are-they-now-paul-horcher/

[177] A Republican, Richard Mountjoy, was elected to both the Senate and the Assembly. By a 40-39 vote, which Mountjoy was not allowed to participate in, he was forced to take his Senate seat. A Republican was later elected to the seat. See Richardson, *Willie Brown,* 377-379, for a discussion of the maneuverings.

[178] "Assemblyman Defeats GOP Recall Attempt," *San Francisco Chronicle* (August 23, 1995).

[179] Horcher was later criticized for receiving a job from Brown when he worked as Mayor of San Francisco.

[180] "Horcher Recalled – Emphatically," *California Journal Weekly* (May 22, 1995).

[181] *Sacramento Bee* (July 2, 1995).

[182] Editorial, "Abuse of the Recall," *San Francisco Chronicle* (August 24, 1995).

[183] "Assemblyman Defeats GOP Recall Attempt," *San Francisco Chronicle* (August 23, 1995).

[184] Charles Price, "Paying the Tab for Recall Elections," *California Journal* (June 1, 1996). While Price points out the other benefits that Republican leaders expected to receive from a successful recall, specifically increased power over a host of local issues, there is little doubt that the reason for the recall was the Speakership fight.

[185] There was approximately twenty-eight percent voter turnout. By the time of the Machado recall vote, Brown was no longer Speaker. Zimmerman, *The Recall,* 85. An additional postscript for the Machado recall was that Machado sought $889,000 in reimbursement for his recall expenses as allowed by California law. Machado request was denied, and he chose not to fight it in court. Sam Stanton, "Davis win could cost state millions," *Sacramento Bee* (July 31, 2003).

display of political power,"[186] he maneuvered to elect Doris Allen, an embittered Republican backbencher, to the Speakership and had himself named to the newly created position of Speaker Emeritus.[187]

Allen was considered "woefully inadequate"[188] by opinion writers, and compared to the "Vichy French"[189] by Republicans. On November 28, 1995, Allen was handily defeated, sixty-five to thirty-five percent, with a turnout around twenty-six percent of registered voters. But before the recall of Allen took place, she gave up the speakership in favor of another Republican, Brian Setencich. He was ousted through parliamentary means and the Republicans finally elected their new party leader, Curt Pringle, as Speaker.

The recall may have gotten the Republicans back in charge, but the cost was very high. They lost the majority in the 1996 elections and have not regained it since; Assemblyman Setencich lost a primary election;[190] aides to the Republican Speaker Pringle were indicted for misuse of offices in the Allen and Horcher recall;[191] Governor Pete Wilson was threatened with a recall campaign by Jesse Jackson that was referred to as a "caricature... of the populist nuttiness in which California's government... has become stuck."[192] Wilson embarked upon a failed presidential run in 1996. The Maestro of the recall fight, former Assembly Speaker Willie Brown, was strengthened by the fight and easily won two terms as Mayor of San Francisco, where he was succeeded by....Gavin Newsom.[193]

Observers were uncertain as to what the future would hold for the recall. During the battles, Mike Schroder, vice chairman of the Republican Party, predicted, "recalls won't be unusual in five years."[194] History proved Schroder wrong on the timing, though perhaps not by much.

Governor Gray Davis

The recall took on new life when it was used to oust the highest-ranking officer in California, Governor Gray Davis, in October 2003. This event, and the subsequent election of actor Arnold Schwarzenegger, stunned Americans, many of whom were caught unaware by the power of the recall. Prior to the Davis recall, there were 36 failed recall attempts against Governors in

---

[186] B. Drummond Ayres Jr., "California Speaker Frustrates G.O.P. One Last Time," *New York Times* (June 6, 1995).
[187] A.G. Block, "A Twisted Tale of Revenge," *California Journal* (January 1, 1996). Allen's discontent with the Republicans was based on Brulte's support for one of her opponents in a primary for a state Senate seat. After Allen's election, Brulte stepped down as Republican leader to run for the state Senate.
[188]"Two-Cents Commentary," *California Journal* (February 1, 1996).
[189]Greg Lucas, "Denouncements of New Assembly Speaker Get Uglier; Republican fax attack fuels rumors," *San Francisco Chronicle* (June 15, 1995).
[190]Mary Lynne Vellinga and Jon Matthews, "Republican Get Their Revenge on 'Traitor' Setencich," *Sacramento Bee* (March 28, 1996).
[191] "3rd Speaker's Aide to admit election fraud; Pringle worker implicated in Allen recall campaign," *San Francisco Chronicle* (March 13, 1996).
[192]Peter Schrag, "Recall Ad Absurdum," *Sacramento Bee* (August 2, 1995).
[193] Note that Brown was term-limited, so leaving the Assembly was going to happen regardless. Brown has to be one of the most famous state legislative leaders of all time. Sam Rayburn and Tip O'Neill went on to become US House Speakers, but I'm not sure who else "broke out." Note also that about the time of these events, Brown was dating future Vice President Kamala Harris.
[194] "The Politics of Recall" *California Journal* (July 1, 1995).

California history.[195]

Why Davis was recalled is not clear. The energy crisis,[196] spawned in part by Enron, was the proximate cause, but in many ways this was the consummate kitchen sink recall. Commentators cited his personality,[197] a failure to properly manage the state's budget,[198] a right-wing conspiracy,[199] or unprecedented voter anger at the political system.[200] Davis' close race (he only won 47%) and his willingness to get involved in the Republican primary to help choose his opponent, was another source of anger. One columnist claimed that Davis was in the pocket of special interests and tied his downfall to the anti-SP movement that begat the recall.[201]

The reaction to the recall petitioning was illustrative of the recall's heretofore-marginal place on the political spectrum. Many commentators expressed shock at the unheralded recall, and ironically, in light of the hyper-democratic anti-recall arguments of Hamilton, Taft and others, complained that the recall itself was an undemocratic device.[202]

The origins of the Davis recall are a matter for some debate. Credit has been awarded to talk radio programs, as a conservative political activist named Ted Costa started the recall on a talk radio show, and other programs were instrumental in rallying support for the petition drive. This was not Costa's first foray into recall politics, as he was a supporter of the Roberti recall, and an opponent of the Machado one.[203] However, some Republican leaders were contemplating a recall before that time, even though the national Republicans appeared to be wary of a potential boomerang effect. [204] Despite the credit these early activists received in later narratives, their efforts seemed to be sputtering,[205] until Republican Representative Darrell Issa pledged over a million dollars to pay for enough signature gatherers necessary to get the measure on the ballot.[206]

---

[195] The first was against Culbert Olson in 1939. The following two Governors (Earl Warren and Goodwin Knight) did not face recall attempts, but every Governor since has faced one.
https://www.sos.ca.gov/elections/recalls/complete-list-recall-attempts Bruce Catton, "California Split Threatens Hopes for Third Term," *Hope Star* March 11, 1940. That is Bruce Catton as a reporter, before his masterpiece "Army of the Potomac" fame.
[196] "Crisis in California," *California Journal* (August 1, 2003).
[197] Tom Chorneau "Davis downfall rooted in his personality and political style," *Associated Press* (October 8, 2003) Matt Welch, "Bad Boys Get Spanked: Recall was about one important issue – firing Gray Davis," *Reason online* (October 9, 2003).
[198] Alan Greenblatt, "Total Recall," *Governing* (September 2003).
[199] Michael Finnegan, "Davis Seeks to Shift Focus to Recall Backers," *Los Angeles Times* (June 24, 2003).
[200] David Lesher, "The Rise of the Voter," *California Journal* (September 2003).
[201] Dan Weintraub, "The Making of a Revolt and a 2-Man Race for Governor," *Sacramento Bee* (October 5, 2003). "Davis had become the modern day equivalent of the California pols who did the railroads bidding."
[202] Mitchell Landsberg, "The Recall Campaign; Question of Fairness," *Los Angeles Times* (September 14, 2003).
[203] Lisa M. Krieger, "Gun Lobby." Kathie A. Smith "Machado Recall Faltering? Richter Questions Wisdom of GOP Effort," *Modesto Bee* (July 25, 1995).
[204] Daniel Weintraub, "Facts and Fiction about the California Recall Election," *Sacramento Bee* (October 7, 2003). Weintraub, "The Making of a Revolt." Megan Garvey, "Talk Radio Beats the Drum for Recall," *Los Angeles Times* (July 27, 2003).
[205] Robert Salladay, "Davis recall drive runs low on funds," *San Francisco Chronicle* (April 27, 2003); Margaret Talev, "Long Road for Davis Recall Try," *Sacramento Bee* (May 11, 2003).
[206] Dan Morain and Gregg Jones, "Rep. Issa Launches New Davis Recall," *Los Angeles Times* (May 6, 2003). Margaret Talev, "California' governor's recall no impulse aim for Rep. Darrell Issa," *Sacramento Bee* (June 16,

1e recall had one big advantage – the 2002 California gubernatorial election had the lowest
)ter turnout for a governor's race in history. Fifty percent of registered voters, and only thirty-
x percent of eligible voters went to the polls that day. Therefore, the number of signatures
:eded to get on the ballot was proportionally lower than ever.

'hen the recall got onto the ballot, candidates of all stripes started entering the race. Minimal
quirements to get placed on the ballot (gathering sixty-five signatures and paying $3,500),
sulted in 135 different candidates entering the race, from former TV Child actor Gary Coleman
porn star Mary Carey, to Hustler publisher Larry Flynt to Arianna Huffington.
t first it looked like the Republican favored candidate would be the former mayor of Los
ngeles Richard Riordan, who lost the Republican nomination in 2002. Davis got involved in
.e nomination battle, spending millions on a campaign to help choose his opponent, the vastly
.ore conservative Bill Simon. In the ensuing year, this tactic (a singular variety of political dirty
cks colorfully known as ratfucking), has become a standard play. But at the time, it was
ocking.

.ordan was counting on the support of Schwarzenegger. But Schwarzenegger surprised
eryone (and destroyed Riordan's campaign) by jumping into the race. Among the other
:publican candidates were Issa, former major league baseball commissioner Peter Ueberroth,
.mon, and conservative state Senator Thomas McClintock.

order to focus the campaign on a partisan angle, Davis attempted to keep the big name
:mocrats, such as Senator Dianne Feinstein, out of the race, though Lieutenant Governor Cruz
istamante, who had an icy relationship with Davis, jumped in. In the end, most of the big name
:publican candidates dropped out before the vote, leaving only Schwarzenegger and
cClintock to battle for the party's base. The Republicans were concerned about the possibility
.at McClintock would siphon support from the far more popular Schwarzenegger, and allow
istamante to triumph, but in the end, such concerns were unfounded.

ithout spending too much time on the twists and turns, there were a number of lawsuits, the
ost interesting one led to a change in the law permitting any voter who casts a ballot against the
:all to be able to vote in the replacement election.
.e recall was eventually held on October 7, 2003, Davis was recalled by fifty-five percent of
e vote, and Schwarzenegger was elected to replace him. Schwarzenegger garnered forty-eight
rcent of the vote, Bustamante received thirty-one percent and McClintock thirteen percent.
xty percent of voters turned out for the election, a significantly larger percentage than had
:cted Davis, although still fewer than had voted in the 2000 presidential election.[207]
e'll get to the other two state Senators to face a recall vote and to the Gavin Newsom one
ortly. First let's look at Wisconsin, as well as the other recalls that took place throughout the
untry.

)3). According to Weintraub, "Facts and Fiction" 900,000 of the 1.6 million signatures for the recall were
hered by paid professionals, rather than volunteers.
3.2 Million Absentee ballots were requested, and according to one report, 2.2 million were returned. However,
re has not been an official number released by the state. Mike Zapler, "Returned absentee ballots hit record
1bers before today's election," *San Jose Mercury News* (October 7, 2003).

Wisconsin: 2011-2012 Scott Walker Recall

While the Gray Davis ouster was a breakout moment for the recall, in many ways it felt like a sui generis event. With the multitude of Hollywood-inspired candidates and the lack of a signature issue, it felt more like a satire of the political process and an old-time "California is crazy" moment[208] than a genuine political earthquake.

The Wisconsin recall was much different, and in many ways, may be a more useful comparison for the 2021 recall of California Governor Gavin Newsom. The 2010 election[209] saw the electoral birth of the Tea Party movement[210] and arguably its effective takeover of the Republicans Party. The campaign funds issue, the focus on pure partisanship and the media attention on one specific issue that helped fuel the recall attempts echo in the events from a much smaller state.

The recall against Wisconsin Governor Scott Walker, Lieutenant Governor Rebecca Kleefisch and 11 members of the state legislature was a straightforward bare-knuckles political battle. For labor unions – the prime backer of the recall campaigns -- this fight was almost a to-the-death struggle. The recalls were, in almost every significant way, a heightened rerun of the 2010 elections.

Once a Republican stronghold in presidential elections and then a state that went with the winner,[211] Wisconsin swung to the Democrats on the presidential level starting in 1988, when it was one of only 10 states to vote for Dukakis, and voted for Democrats in every election till 2016. On the state level, there was frequent change of control between the parties and, according to one former Senate Majority Leader who joined a previous Republican administration, a long history of bipartisanship.[212]

After two successive Democratic electoral triumphs on the national scene, the 2010 election represented a roaring back for Republicans, especially their most conservative wing. On the national scene, they recaptured the House, winning a net of 63 seats and cut the Democrats' lead in the Senate from 60 to a precarious 53 seats. On the state level, Republicans also romped, taking a net of 4 Governor's seats and 18 houses of state legislatures.

Arguably nowhere was the Republican victory as big as in Wisconsin. U.S. Senator Russell Feingold was defeated in his quest for a fourth term – the only incumbent US Senator to lose office that year – and the Democrats lost two Congressional seats. On the state level, the victory was even greater. The Republicans reversed the Democrats complete control of the state

---

[208] See Michael Lewis, "The Personal is the Antipolitical," *New York Times Magazine*, September 28, 2003. http://www.nytimes.com/2003/09/28/magazine/the-personal-is-the-antipolitical.html?pagewanted=all&src=pm
[209] Due to the overwhelming focus on Presidents, the historical import of mid-term elections get short-shrift. The critical 1896 election should be seen in light of the more dramatic 1894 results. The 1994 mid-term reshaped the Republican Party for a generation to come.
[210] While there are a number of political movements that aligned together, the failures of the Republicans in 2000s may have led to the growth of the Tea Party as a movement.
[211] From its founding in 1864, it only voted twice for Democrats (1892 and 1912) before the New Deal. After that, went with the winner (except in 1944 and 1960) until 1988.
[212] Senator Tim Cullen, Ringside Seat: Wisconsin Politics, the 1970s to Scott Walker, Little Creek Politics , 2015

government, winning the Governor's office for the first time in eight years and taking charge of both houses of the legislature.

Newly elected Governor Scott Walker,[213] with the solid backing of the legislatures, took this victory as a strong mandate to adopt wide-ranging changes to existing government policy. Along with a host of tax and spending cuts and a very powerful gerrymandering map for the state legislature, the administration also pushed forward a proposal removing collective bargaining rights for public sector employees. This last move was thought to be a potentially lethal blow to the core of the union movement.

The issue of removing collective bargaining rights for workers was very popular for Republicans in the aftermath of the 2010 election.[214] In the wake of the recession, Governors knew they had to slash budgets, and the government payroll and especially the benefits packages provided to workers were considered to be one of the easiest targets. At least 18 states proposed eliminating or substantially cutting back public employees' right to collective bargaining. Protests were everywhere, but Wisconsin was the state that stood out.

Why Wisconsin:

There were a few reasons that Wisconsin became the epicenter of the union protests to changes in the collective bargaining law.[215] Some of the other states, such as Alaska, Oklahoma, Kansas, were strongly pro-Republican – to such a degree that a concentrated action by unions would have a very limited effect or would have backfired entirely. Other states, such as Ohio, saw protests, but there was no mechanism to remove the leadership.

Others states, such as California (and non-recall New York), were led by Democratic Governors. While the unions were upset with the policies of these Democratic Governors, they were vastly preferable to the Republican alternative. Protest occurred, but negotiation was clearly the best path going forward.

All of these factors left two states as the best possible targets for action– Wisconsin and Michigan. And Wisconsin was a better target. This may seem odd, as Michigan has a very strong union movement and has a deeper connection with the recall than Wisconsin.[216] On the local level, in 2011 Michigan held the most recalls of any state. It also had four state level recalls since 1983. There was a petition campaign against Governor Rick Snyder in 2011, which got 500,000 signatures, but this was nowhere near the 807,000 valid signatures needed to get it on the ballot.

This exemplified the fact that for a recall petition to succeed in Michigan, many more signatures were needed there than in Wisconsin. The two states' laws required the same percentage of

---

Walker's career took off due to a recall effort against Milwaukee County Executive F. Thomas Ament in 2002 over new pension rules for county workers. Ament resigned and then-Assemblyman Walker won the special to replace him. Jason Stein and Patrick Marley's, More than they Bargained For: Scott Walker, Unions and the Fight Wisconsin, University of Wisconsin Press, 2013, 19.
Michael Cooper and Katharine Q. Seelye, "Wisconsin Leads Way as Workers Fight State Cuts," New York Times, February 18, 2011. http://www.nytimes.com/2011/02/19/us/politics/19states.html?pagewanted=all
http://www.nytimes.com/2011/02/19/us/19union.html?ref=politics
http://www.huffingtonpost.com/2012/11/07/michigan-proposal-2-results-2012_n_2080767.html

signatures and those Michigan petitioners had 30 more days than Wisconsin's to collect them (that law has since been changed). But Michigan is a much larger state than Wisconsin, so the absolute number of signatures was nearly double.

But the bigger reason may have been more fundamental. And as we will continually see, the vagaries of the recall law play a major role in its use.

Under Michigan law at the time (it has since been changed), recalls for state level officials were a two-vote process. Unlike in California, North Dakota or Wisconsin, the first vote took place on an election or primary day or on the designated special election date. If the candidate was removed, then the next vote would not take place for months. If Snyder would have been recalled in November, the replacement vote would not take place until February. In that time, the Lieutenant Governor (also a Republican) would serve. It would be possible to try and recall the Lieutenant Governor, but the entire line of succession, including the leaders of both houses of the legislature, were also Republican. The chance of recalling enough people to actually get a Democrat in office was very small.

Additionally, the two-step Michigan recall process meant that Democrats would have had to win two elections. First, they would have to win the recall, then the replacement race. As we'll see, in 2011, a Republican legislator was recalled and then replaced by another Republican.
Wisconsin was a different story. It also had a strong pro-union history – in fact, it had been the first state to mandate collective bargaining for public sector workers.[217] Madison, its capital city, is considered one of the most liberal cities in the US,[218] and is also home to the state university flagship. Therefore, it was much easier to draw a large crowd for protests at the capital buildings, making it into a bigger story. It also had a much smaller population than Michigan, thus a much lower absolute signature total. Wisconsin also has a very unusual provision discussed in its origin history, allowing any eligible voter signatures to count. In other jurisdictions, it is limited to registered voters. This difference allows many more signatures to get through and limits the success of challenges.

The result was that the anti-collective bargaining plan resulted in a strong pushback by the unions. Tens of thousands of union members and their supporters descended on the state Capital in Madison for multi-day protests. Coverage was intense, though there was a heavy gloss depending on which side was covering the story. MSNBC's Ed Schultz made it his big issue,[219] while Fox News took a strong pro-Walker slant.

The Wisconsin state legislature became a national story. However, these protests were of limited value. In the State Assembly, the Democrats were heavily outnumbered. In the Senate, the Democrats had one weapon in their arsenal. The Senate was split 19-14. But to vote on these changes, the Republicans needed a two-thirds quorum in session. So while they had the votes,

---

[217] Joseph McCartin, "What's really going on in Wisconsin?" *The New Republic*, February 19, 2011. http://www.tnr.com/article/politics/83829/wisconsin-public-employees-walker-negotiate#
[218] Sewell Chan, "Name America's Most Liberal City," *New York Times*, November 21, 2007. http://cityroom.blogs.nytimes.com/2007/11/21/name-americas-most-liberal-city/
[219] David Zurawick, "Ed Schultz, MSNBC lead TV way on important Wisconsin recall story," *Baltimore Sun*, August 9, 2011 http://articles.baltimoresun.com/2011-08-09/entertainment/bal-ed-schultz-msnbc--wisconsin-scot walker-recall-story-20110809_1_ed-schultz-wisconsin-msnbc

they needed at least one Democrat in attendance. In order to stop this action, the entire Democratic delegation fled the state.[220] The Republican leader threatened arrest and other actions, but it was only after some negotiations that the Democrats returned.[221] In the end, the anti-collective bargaining law was enacted virtually without change.

In the past, these protests might have been the beginning and the end of the fight. But now, both sides immediately looked to the recall to gain a political advantage. While the Republicans were initially threatening the recall against the Senators who fled the state, it was the unions who were the prime movers in putting recalls on the ballot.

However, due to a quirk in Wisconsin law, the recall would be very limited in its use. As discussed above, Wisconsin's law prevented any recalls from beginning until the official had served one year on the term. It is the only state that has a year-long grace period for newly elected officials (others have between three months and six months, while some jurisdictions have the opposite law, no recalls in the last year).

For the Assembly members, who served two-year terms, the recall would be effectively useless. The Assembly was strongly Republican, and the Democrats had only 39 of the 99 seats. For Walker and the half of the Senate elected in 2010, they had a year's respite from facing a recall vote. Therefore, the only officials who could face a recall in 2011, while passions were at their highest, were the Senators elected in 2008.

The reality was therefore clear that the recall campaign in the Senate could only be of limited value to the Democrats. Even if they recaptured the Senate, they would have only gained at best a blocking position. It was clear they would not be able to propose any legislation that would pass both the assembly and Walker's veto, nor would they be able to overturn Walker's new union law.

Despite this limited value, practically every Senator eligible to face a recall was threatened with one. After the 60-day signature gathering campaign, nine of the recalls got on the ballot – six against Republicans and three against Democrats.
Another quirk of Wisconsin recall law is that it has a primary election attached. The result meant that if two candidates from the same party were running in the recall, the recall would be delayed for a month and half. Additionally, since Wisconsin is an open primary state, voters could come out and vote in the other party's primary and try to choose a lesser candidate for the election. If there was no primary vote, the election immediately would move to the general election stage, which would have cut back on the Republicans' time to fundraise.

The impact of the combination of these factors on the election was very seriously threatening to the Republicans, who did their best to buy time with countermeasures. They put up primary candidates against eight of the nine Democrats running.[222] These candidates were so-called "fake

---

[20]Jeff Mayers, "Democrats flee Wisconsin to protest union curbs," *Reuters*, February 17, 2011. ttp://www.reuters.com/article/2011/02/18/us-wisconsin-protests-idUSTRE71H01920110218
[1] Cullen, 15-17. Cullen, a former Democratic Majority Leader in the Senate, notes that his party did not seem to ave much of a plan once they fled the state.
[2] A Republican assemblyman failed to turn in the signatures necessary to get on the ballot for the ninth Senate seat.

Democrats." They also didn't put up much of a race in the election, but they did buy the Republicans more time to fundraise and to campaign against the recall.

The Republicans also tried using a bit of timing to their potential advantage in the recall. The recalls against two of the sitting Democrats were scheduled weeks after the ones against the six Republicans. The Republicans probably hoped to take advantage of this time lag to recapture the Senate in these two races after most of the races were over and excitement waned.

The actual campaigns turned out quite different than observers may have expected. "Ironically, the recall campaigns included little discussion of collective bargaining, the issue that gave rise to them. Democrats focused on issues with wider traditional resonance for voters, such as Walker's cuts to education and health care. Republicans were no more eager to broach the subject of their controversial action, talking instead more generally of their efforts to hold down taxes and spending. The recall took on the tint of ordinary, albeit unusually expensive and slick, campaigns."[223]

The final races were held on different days. The three Democrats easily won. On July 19, Senator Dave Hansen won his race with 63% in his favor. On August 16, Senator Jim Holperin beat back his second recall election, with a 55%-45% margin, and Senator Robert Wirch won 57%-43%.

The Republican races, all on August 9, presented a different story. The Democrats needed to win three seats to flip the chamber. They only got two. Senators Robert Cowles and Sheila Harsdorf both easily won with 57% and 58% respectively. The Democrats had hoped for a better result against Alberta Darling and Luther Olsen, but each of those Republicans skated by. Darling had a particularly good race. She had won office in 2008 by a single percent. In the recall, she took 54% of the vote, while Olsen won by only 52-48%.

The Democrats' big win saw Jennifer Shilling take out Senator Dan Kapanke 55-45%. Shilling and Kapanake had a rematch in 2016, with Shilling once again winning, although it went to a recount. Kapanke also lost another nail biter in 2020 for the same seat (this time against Shilling's replacement, Brad Pfaff).[224]

The other race was a rerun, with Republican Senator Randy Hopper losing to Democrat Jessica King, who he had previously beaten by only 163 votes in 2008. Hopper lost by only a little over 2%. Hopper had what can charitably be called a difficult campaign – he faced a divorce, infidelity charges and claims (unproven) that he helped his mistress gain a higher salary in a state job.

The minimal long-term impact of these races can be seen by the 2012 general election result.

---

[223] Stein and Marley,269.

[224] Olivia Herken," Brad Pfaff Claims victory in close Senate Distrct 32 race, recount a possibility," November 4, 2020, *LaCrosse Tribune*. Note that if Kapanake had won, the Republicans would have gained a Supermajority in the Senate, a sign of how it changed in the ensuing decade. https://lacrossetribune.com/community/brad-pfaff-claims-victory-in-close-senate-district-32-race-recount-a-possibility/article_8bed2936-2bec-5194-a66c-dd24a39c1448.htm

With the seats newly gerrymandered, King lost her re-election race. Holperin did not run for re-election, but was replaced by a Republican.

The Republicans claimed victory by keeping the Senate, though losing two seats did still sting. More important than the loss of two Senate seats (which proved temporary), the recalls laid out the tactics and strategies that would be seen in 2012. And the one that counted the most was money. It was easily the most expensive race in the country. The Wisconsin Democracy Project broke down the figures.[225]

The total campaign spending for the nine 2011 recalls was estimated to be $44 million. By comparison, $20 million was dropped on all the Wisconsin legislative races in 2010, and $37.4 million on the Governor's races. Three candidates broke the previous record of $722,333 spent in one race. Senator Alberta Darling spent a record $1.23 million in her successful race. The other two were losers. Republican Senator Dan Kapanke spent $1.05 million and Darling's challenger Democratic Representative Sandra Pasch spent $800,744.

But those figures only tell a small part of the story. It was spending by outside groups that was the real driving factor in the recall. In the 2011 recall, they spent an estimated $34.6 million. As the Wisconsin Democracy Campaign noted:

The groups' spending in the recalls also was nearly five times more than the previous record $7.1 million spent by outside groups in all of the 115 legislative races in 2008. It also eclipses all outside group spending in the 1998, 2002, 2006 and 2010 races for governor combined, which totaled about $28.9 million.

Six of the nine recall races beat the previous record $3 million spent by the candidates and outside groups in a legislative race – the 10th Senate District contest in 2000 won by Republican Sheila Harsdorf who was among the nine recall targets. In addition, the estimated $2 million spent by groups in the 2000 race – the previous record spending by outside groups in a legislative race – was exceeded in seven of the recall races where outside special interests spent between $2.2 million and $7.9 million.[226]

The outside spending presaged the 2012 recalls, as well as the outside spending in the 2012 presidential election. Though, as opposed to the 2012 recall, the biggest outside spender was a Democratic group:

Special interest group spending was led by We Are Wisconsin, a political action committee that spent a record $10.75 million for an electioneering group to support Democrats in the nine races. The PAC was funded by a coalition of unions mostly based in Washington, including the AFL-CIO, the American Federation of State, County and Municipal Employees and the Service Employees International Union, among others. The group sponsored more than 20 television ads in the recall races and spent the most – $2.6 million – to support Pasch in her effort to unseat Darling.

"Groups, Candidates Spend Record $44 Million in Recalls," *WISCDC*, March 12, 2012. p://www.wisdc.org/pr092011.php
WISDC.

2012 – Walker Redux

The senatorial recalls of 2011 were an expensive prelude to the even bigger show that was coming up – the recall campaign against Scott Walker, Lieutenant Governor Rebecca Kleefisch and four Republican state Senators. The issues were much the same, with an added charge of corruption against Walker.

The Walker campaign was set to begin once he was in office a year. With great fanfare, the reca supporters took out petitions in November to start gathering signatures. In a sign of things to come, the union-backers were slightly late to the game, and were not the first group to take out petitions against Walker. One week before the union campaign an unknown group led by donor to the Republican Party took out petitions to recall Walker. The reason for this was clear – it would start the clock for Walker to start raising unlimited funds to fend off the recall campaign.

The recall campaigns also included a debate on whether there had to be a separate recall campaign against Lieutenant Governor Rebecca Kleefisch. Wisconsin is a state with a joint tick for Governor,[227] so one theory held that if Walker was removed, Kleefisch would also be automatically ousted. The pro-recall team wisely decided against testing this theory in court and had a separate recall campaign against Kleefisch.

Also facing recalls were Senate Majority Leader Scott Fitzgerald and Senators Terry Moulton, Pam Galloway and Van Wanggaard. The recalls against all four got on the ballot.
As in the 2011 recall fights, the collective bargaining issue was not the center of attention. Walker tried to make the recall about jobs, and the Democrats focused on an investigation by th Milwaukee County District Attorney over illegal campaign coordination. The investigation had been ongoing since right before his election as governor in 2010 and would not wrap up until 2014.[228]

Walker and his Republican allies looked to muddy the waters of the recall effort at each stage. Multiple reports came out criticizing the signature gathering effort, with complaints that the petitioners would be gathering fraudulent signatures signed by "Mickey Mouse" and others. Unlike in California, the names of the signers were public, which resulted in one judge later losing re-election for signing the petitions.[229]

Wisconsin's Government Accountability Board (GAB) announced that it would not automatically strike fraudulent and duplicative signatures. Walker's team only had 10 days to review signatures. They tried to shift the burden to the recall proponents' review for the purpos

---

[227] In an attempt on cornering the market on esoteric subjects, I wrote a paper on the value of a same-ticket versus separately elected Lieutenant Governors. I haven't kept it up, but my research showed that separately elected Governors are vastly more likely to have an ongoing political career. Joshua Spivak "Splitting the Ticket: New Yc Should Separately Elect Lieutenant Governor," Wagner College, June 23 2010 https://www.slideshare.net/WagnerCollegeNYC/splitting-the-ticket. Also Joshua Spivak "Elect Lieutenant Gover Directly," *New York Daily News*, March 10, 2010.
[228] Jason Stein and Patrick Marley's "More than they Bargained For: Scott Walker, Unions and the Fight for Wisconsin," University of Wisconsin Press, 2013 is an excellent account of the complex issues surrounding Walk
[229] Judge Tom Wolfram -- http://archive.jsonline.com/news/ozwash/ozaukee-judge-wolfgram-appears-to-be-ouste 6e9cr5g-201166271.html/

of striking signatures. After much back-and-forth, this ended up being just a tactic in the larger fight. Petitioners handed in 931,053 signatures and 900,938 were found valid – a 3.2% failure rate. They only needed 540,000. Walker and his supporters did not waste time challenging the signatures.[230]

In what would prove to be a go-to tactic for Republicans in the future, Walker, future RNC Chairman (and future U.S. Chief of Staff) Reince Preibus[231] and future Speaker of the Assembly Robin Vos made false claims of voter fraud. Walker claimed that he would need 53% of the vote total to win (which was exactly the total he got in the end),[232] and later claimed fraud in the Senate victory for the Democrats. Interestingly enough, Vos' estranged wife faced charges that she voted in the recall despite being a resident of Idaho.[233] The one actual fraud charges brought was against a Walker supporter who voted five times. There was also a bizarre 2016 claim by Trump/Nixon Henchman Roger Stone that Walker won through fraud.[234]

The campaign was set for May 15 for the primary and June 6 for the general election. An Occupy Madison protestor named Arthur Kohl-Riggs, who frequently dressed up in an Abraham Lincoln costume, ran in the Republican Primary.[235] Walker actually did very well in the primary – turnout in his uncompetitive race almost equaled the Democratic one (Walker got 626,538 votes. Five Democrats totaled 670,278), which should have served as a warning sign for what was to come.

The Democrats had a significant battle for the nomination, featuring Milwaukee Mayor Thomas Barrett, who Walker beat in 2010, former Dane County Executive Kathleen Falk, state Senator Kathleen Vinhout and Secretary of State Doug La Follette.[236] Falk had the strong backing of the unions in the state, but Barrett easily triumphed, gaining 58% of the vote in the primary.[237] Stein and Marley note that the high cost of the primary (with labor spending $4.5 million to elect Falk) drained Barrett's coffers just when he needed the money the most.[238]

The actual election was somewhat anticlimactic. The polls showed a close race, but with Walker leading in most polls. The polls did well in predicting the race. As with the other gubernatorial recalls, turnout shot up. Walker did a half a percent better than in 2010, garnering 53.08% of the vote. Kleefisch had a similar result, taking 52.9%.

---

[230] There were five clearly fake names: Adolf Hitler, Mick E. Mous, Donald L. Duck, Fungky Van Den Elzen and I Love Scott Walker Thanks.

[231] http://www.jsonline.com/news/statepolitics/rnc-chairman-priebus-alleges-rampant-vote-fraud-2f5jud3-55817075.html

[232] Stephen Hayes, "High Noon in Wisconsin," *Weekly Standard*, May 28, 2012. https://www.washingtonexaminer.com/weekly-standard/high-noon-in-wisconsin

[233] Heather Asiyanbi, "Update: Vos Attorney Responds to Voter Fraud Complaint," *Patch*, September 29, 2012. ttps://patch.com/wisconsin/mountpleasant/voter-fraud-complaint-now-with-district-attorney-s-office

[234] Roger Stone, "Can the 2016 election be rigged? You bet," *The Hill*, August 16, 2016. ttps://thehill.com/blogs/pundits-blog/presidential-campaign/291534-can-the-2016-election-be-rigged-you-bet

[] The Republicans did miss a chance to end the Kleefisch recall early. Turnout for the primary for the Lieutenant overnor was half that of the Governor. The Democrats nominated Firefighter Chief Mahlon Mitchell.

[] Doug La Follette's great-grandfather was apparently Senator Robert "Fighting Bob" La Follete's brother.

During the campaign, Barrett was actually attacked at a County Fair, though it seemed not to have anything to do th the recall.

Stein and Marley, 286.

The Senate races turned out a little different. Senate Majority Leader Scott Fitzgerald and Senators Terry Moulton both easily won. Senator Pam Galloway decided not to run in the replacement race, but a different Republican, State Representative Jerry Petrowski, ran instead and easily won.

The fourth recall, Senator Van Wanggaard, turned into a barnburner. Former Senator John Lehman, who ran and lost to Wanggaard in 2010, decided to run against him in the recall. Lehman topped Wanggaard, winning by 819 votes, or a little over 1%. Vos again got into the act, claiming fraud because the race was run under the old district lines, not the newly drawn one.[239]

The Lehman victory flipped control of the Senate to the Democrats, but this was a very hollow victory. The Democrats only had control for six months when little was happening. In the 2012 election, despite Barack Obama winning Wisconsin, the newly gerrymandered district lines worked against the Democrats, who went from a 17-16 majority to an 18-15 minority.

In 2014, Wanggard reclaimed his seat. Lehman decided not to run in the newly redistricted seat and instead moved up – he was the Democrat's Lieutenant Governor Nominee in the losing race to Walker.

The impact was felt for years. The Government Accountability Board, considered one of the best electoral regulators in the country, was effectively destroyed. The state was bitterly politically divided.

The recall may have greatly benefited Walker. He was now a national figure, one that led him to make a serious, albeit brief, run for the presidency. While Midwest Governors are always seen as prime presidential contenders,[240] there were plenty of those from larger states. But Walker received an enormous amount of attention, far eclipsing what other governors would get for anything other than a scandal or a serious presidential campaign. In a quick search of *The New York Times* (*NYT*) and *The Wall Street Journal* (*WSJ*) from February 5, 2011 to December 31, 2012, Scott Walker was mentioned in 422 *New York Times* and 667 *Wall Street Journal* stories.

Compare that to some of his fellow GOP governors who were elected at the exact same time from much larger states with far greater economic impact on the country. Ohio's John Kasich received mentions in 64 *NYT* and 167 *WSJ* pieces. Michigan's Rick Snyder saw his name in 105 *NYT* and 196 *WSJ* stories. Florida's Rick Scott was mentioned 214 times by the *NYT* and 152 times by the *WSJ*. And Pennsylvania's Tom Corbett appeared in 68 *NYT* and 117 *WSJ* articles.[241]

---

[239] https://www.wispolitics.com/index.iml?Article=272603
[240] Perhaps unjustifiably so – it may just be a Gilded Age remembrance. McKinley was the last Midwestern governor elected president. Since then only three have even received the nomination – James Cox in 1920, Alfred Landon in 1936 and Adlai Stevenson in 1952 and 1956. Two of those were among the biggest blowouts in history.
[241] Joshua Spivak, "How Scott Walker Got his Head Start," *Newsweek*, March 1, 2015. http://www.newsweek.com/how-scott-walker-got-his-head-start-310265. At the time, I thought he made vastly mo sense as a VP pick that Paul Ryan (allowing Romney to play against the unions). Was I right? No idea, but I wasn' wrong.

North Dakota Governor/AG/Agriculture Commissioner Recalls: 1921 was a good year (for recalls)

North Dakota stands out not only for its role as the first state to have a gubernatorial recall, but the only one to take out three state-wide officials in that one fateful day. Unlike the other major recalls, it was an intra-party fight. North Dakota's Governor served a two year term. In his detailed looked at the North Dakota recall, Professor David Schecter notes that "there has been no complete evaluation of the Frazier race…"[242] This evaluation relies heavily on Schecter's work.

In 1916, the Nonpartisan League, which was compromised of Progressive Republicans and some Democrats, created an "advocated state ownership of elevators, mills, and the like along with state hail insurance and reasonably run banks." [243] The grain elevator companies were a powerful player in a state with 70% farmers. Governor Lynn Frazier won office on the NPL line.

Opposing Frazier was the Independent Voters Association, which Schecter notes, dropped the "Republican" from their name to appeal to a broader audience. Frazier won re-election in 2018 with 60% of the vote.

During the next session of the legislature, North Dakota adopted a recall law. The legislatures approved it on March 6, 1919 and the Constitutional Amendment was overwhelmingly passed by the voters on March 16, 1920, 63%-37%.
In 1920, trouble started piling up for the NPL. The NPL was starting to splinter and a drought hit North Dakota's economy in 1920. Frazier won re-election, but barely, with 51-49% and the NPL lost control of the House. The next term went poorly, as claims of mismanagement and corruption hit state-supported enterprises, including the state bank, a mill and the state's Home Building Association.

The IVA took aim at the state's Industrial Commission, which oversaw the state-sponsored entities and was a composed of Frazier, Attorney General William Lemke and Commissioner of Agriculture and Labor John Hagen. Petitioners got 74,000 signatures, and nominated Ragnvold Nestos for Governor, Sveinbjorn Johnson for AG and Joseph Kitchen for Commissioner of Agriculture and Labor.

Nestos was seen as a more liberal member of the IVA and his Scandinavian background was a strong positive in the state.

The vote, a special election held on October 21, 1921, was focused on mismanagement and potential corruption. There were also claims of being close to the more radical union group, the Industrial Workers of the World – the famed Wobblies. The actual state entities were still a net positive, and the campaign did not focus on them. A late-breaking injunction issued by the

[12] David Schecter, "California's Right of Removal: Recall Politics in the Modern Era," *California Politics & Policy*, December 2008, 2 at
ttp://www.fresnostate.edu/socialsciences/polisci/documents/CaliforniasRightofRemoval.pdf
[3] Schecter, 6

judiciary stopped the Bank of North Dakota from operating, which helped turn the tide against Frazier.

The election was super close, and almost a full inversion of the 1920 race. Frazier lost to Nestos 51-49% (106,332-111,4340). Lemke and Hagen also lost by about the same totals. Yet despite this, Schecter notes that on the same day, state voters approved seven measures that backed up the NPL program.

Nestos went on to win one more term in office. Frazier, Lemke and Hagen came back and… well, we get to them in our comeback stories.

Arizona: The Recall of '88 That never happened

Neither Arizona nor Oregon held an actual recall election of a Governor but both are worth talking about.

In 1988, Arizona Governor Evan Meacham should have faced a recall election, but the legislature managed to jump in front of the vote. Meacham was targeted for a host of reasons, including preventing the declaration of the Martin Luther King Jr. holiday, addressing the John Birch Society and a slew of objectionable comments. Additionally, he was indicted on six felony charges over a joint loan with a developer. Petitioners got over 300,000 signatures (they needed 216,000) but the day the recall was approved, Meacham was impeached and convicted by the legislature for making death threats against grand jury witnesses and misusing state funds. The Supreme Court ruled in April that the impeachment took precedence, and ordered the recall cancelled.[244]

Oregon in 2015: Recall leads to Resignation:

In 2015, right after winning his fourth term as governor, John Kitzhaber (D) faced a major scandal involving his fiancée's efforts to seemingly monetize the state's highest office. Kitzhaber was hit with two recall petitions, one started by two of the leading strategists for Kitzhaber's most recent Republican opponent. Petitioners would have needed over 220,000 signatures to get the recall on the ballot, and Kitzhaber had the advantage of a grace period. Oregon law does not allow any collection of signatures until the official has served in office at least six months in office of his or her current term. However, he had two problems that invited a recall effort. Oregon has no impeachment procedure, making a recall the only way to get him out. And his replacement would be a fellow Democrat, Secretary of State Kate Brown, not a Republican. This meant that Democrats could feel free to sign for his ouster. Two petitions were being taken out when Kitzhaber resigned.[245]

The Rest: All 21 Other State-Level Recalls In US History

Before jumping into the legislature, in on May 19, 1922 in Oregon, two public service commissioners, Fred Buchtel and Fred Williams, were kicked out office in a recall vote. The

---

[244] Zimmerman, 67-68.
[245] Lee Van Der Voo and Kirk Johnson, "Gov. John Kitzhaber of Oregon Resigns Amid Crisis," *New York Times*, February 13, 2015.

recall was over a telephone rate increase. [246]

1932: Wisconsin State Senator Otto Mueller: Mueller got into a fight with Governor Phillip La Follette over a tax bill. Christian Schneider notes that the recall was "part of a larger effort to remove state officials who opposed a tax bill..." with petitions taken out against three other Senators).[247] Mueller easily won the recall vote, getting over 62 percent.

1935 Oregon State Representative Howard Merriam: Merriam opposed the Townsend Plan, a popular pre-Social Security idea that would provide a $200 monthly pension for everyone over 60. Merriam's vote opposition led to a recall vote and his ouster.[248] Not sure what the totals are.

1971 Idaho State Senator Fisher Ellsworth and Assemblyman Alden Hyde were recalled because they supported a pay raise; Again, there is not much on this one. Idaho did not have a replacement race.

1981 Washington State Senator Peter Von Reichbauer: After his election as a Democrat, Von Reichbauer switched parties. This resulted in the Republicans flipping the chamber and getting a 25-24 majority in the Senate. Washington State's Malfeasance Standard laws were much less severe – a 1983 court ruling cut back on the ability to have a recall. Von Reichbauer survived the recall vote. He is still in office as a member of the Kings County Council.

1983 – Michigan State Senator Phil Mastin and David Serotkin: Mastin (D) and Serotkin (D) both voted for a tax hike. Petitioners launched a recall effort against both Senators and Governor James Blanchard (D). Mastin and Serotkin lost their recall elections overwhelmingly. Both apparently outspent the pro-recall group by a margin of 10-1. Serotkin resigned before certification in an attempt to be a candidate in the replacement race (the Attorney General ruled against this move). Both were replaced by Republicans. The two removals flipped the chamber to GOP control, which they have not relinquished since.[249]

1985 – Oregon State Representative Pat Gillis: Gillis (R) falsely claimed that he earned a Master's Degree. He also falsified campaign endorsements. He was later acquitted of all charges, but not before being kicked out in a recall vote.

1988 – Oregon State Senator Bill Olson: Olson (R), who had a record of "fighting abortion and child pornography," pled guilty to second degree sex assault with a 13 year old female relative. He lost by a 3-2 margin, though apparently he was "very pleased" because he got more votes than he thought he would get.[250] He was replaced by a Republican.

1990 Wisconsin Assemblyman Jim Holperin: Holperin, the only state legislator to face and win

Merton K. Cameron, "The Experience of Oregon with Popular Election and Recall of Public Service Commissioners, *The Journal of Land & Public Utility Economics*, February 1929, 48-61.
Christian Schneider, "The History of the Recall in Wisconsin," *WPRI Report*, April 2012.
Oregon History Project at https://www.oregonhistoryproject.org/articles/historical-records/news-article-smith-asts-at-new-deal/#.YMhbv_IKhPY
Ken Braun, "Total Recall – Michigan Tax Revolts 1983 and Today" *Michigan Capitol Confidential*, April 1, 08. https://www.michigancapitolconfidential.com/9334
Susan Tebbe, "State Senator, admitted child abuser, recalled," *UPI Archives*, March 23, 1988.
ps://www.upi.com/Archives/1988/03/23/State-senator-admitted-child-abuser-recalled/9215575096400/

two recall elections, survived his first with 61% of the vote in his favor. The recall was over votes on tribal fishing rights.

1994-1995—California. See above.

1996 Wisconsin State Senator George Petak – Perhaps the paradigmatic recall. Petak reversed his vote on a tax to build Miller Stadium and keep the Brewers in Milwaukee. This led to an immediate eruption of voter anger, and Petak was kicked out in a 51-49% vote. Petak's ouster resulted in the chamber flipping control from Republican to Democrat.

2003 Wisconsin State Senator Gary George – George, who had served in the Senate for 23 years, faced a recall after he voted against a bill supporting a casino expansion in Milwaukee (The bill was backed by the Democratic Governor). George was also the target of an investigation into a kickback scheme, which led to his pleading out and serving four years in federal prison. George lost the recall vote on October 21, 2003 with only 35% in his favor. Turnout was 8%. However, he was replaced by a fellow Democrat.

2008 California State Senator Jeff Denham – Denham (R) was targeted for a recall officially because he voted against the budget bill, but there was a bigger issue at play. If the Denham was ousted and replaced by a Democrat, the party would have a veto proof majority in both houses of the legislature. This position was bolstered by the fact that the recall effort was launched with the strong support of Senate President Pro Tempore Don Perata (D). After quite a bit of bad press, the Democrats effectively abandoned the campaign, though not before it got on the ballot. Denham easily won, with 75% of the vote in his favor. For Denham, the recall can be seen as a net positive. In 2010, he was elected to Congress.

2008 Michigan House Speaker Andy Dillon – Dillon faced a recall vote over his support for increases in the taxes. The Dillon recall really stands out, as it was held on Election Day. Therefore, he faced both a recall vote and a re-election at the same election. Therefore, the recall would have only removed him for a few months. Regardless he won easily. Interestingly enough, he did slightly better in the general election vote than in the recall. We'll discuss this a bit later, but the totals were14,257-23,987 in the recall, and in the general election, 14,311-27,864,[251] though he later came in a distance second in the Democratic primary for Governor in 2010.

2011-2012 Wisconsin – See above.

2011 Arizona Senate President Russell Pearce – Pearce was the lead sponsor of Arizona's 2010 anti-illegal immigrant law, among other proposals that were seen as very popular among the more right-wing groups. A lawsuit led to the Arizona Supreme Court ruling that the recall was a important right and the state must use a much more lenient "substantial compliance" standard when they are judging signatures. The district was quite Republican, so another Republican, Jerry Lewis, ran in the replacement race. Lewis and Pearce were both members of the Church o the Latter-day Saints, which was a source of significant discussion, including a belief that churc

---

[251] https://mielections.us/election/results/08GEN/#; https://www.waynecounty.com/elected/clerk/november-8-200 general.aspx

members were embarrassed by Pearce. Pearce's team helped back another candidate to draw support away from Lewis. All of this failed, as Pearce was ousted in the recall, 43.5% - 55.1% for Lewis. Pearce followed this up with a quick victory as GOP State Vice Chair, but then ran again for the Senate in a different district in 2012, but lost badly. Lewis also lost the re-election in 2012, though, in a sign of changes in the district and in Arizona at large, he was defeated by a Democrat.

2011 Michigan State Representative Paul Scott – Scott was the Chair of the House Education Committee, where he helped push changes in collective bargaining agreement and in education funding. 20 state legislators were threatened with a recall, but only Scott got to the ballot. The Michigan Education Association (the teachers' union) helped push for the recall. This recall needed the Michigan Supreme Court to step in to order the recall (Scott tried to force it onto a Republican Presidential Primary date, which would have undoubtedly helped him, as there was no Democratic Primary of note). Scott lost the recall by a very slim margin, 50.5%-49.5% -- a total of 232 votes. The replacement race wasn't held until months later, and Scott was replaced by Republican Joe Graves, so the impact was minimal. However, in 2012 after the recall and after the Wisconsin ones, Michigan made significant changes to its recall law (a last moment law that was effectively hidden from view), including a "clarity/factualness" hearing, which has cut down greatly on recalls in Michigan. The law also effectively took the Governor out of the line of fire. Any Governor facing a recall is replaced as provided by law – the Lieutenant Governor takes over.

2013 Colorado Senate President John Morse and Senator Angela Giron – After the "Dark Knight" shooting in a movie theater in Aurora, Colorado passed new gun control laws and Senate Majority Leader John Morse introduced the ban on assault weapons. As with the Roberti recall, local gun groups pushed the recall effort (the NRA originally seemed lukewarm or opposed to the effort). Petitioners managed to get enough signatures to get a recall against Morse and Giron on the ballot, with two others against Senator Evie Hudak and Representative Mike McLachlan failing to get enough signatures. The Giron recall used a new technology that allowed petitioners to check signatures on a smartphone, resulting in an amazingly low 6% failure rate.

Morse lost the recall by a small margin, 51-49%. Giron lost by a bit more 56-44%, though there seemed to be a belief that Giron was simply not liked in the district. Both were replaced by Republicans. Due to a provision in Colorado law, Hudak resigned and was replaced by a Democrat. In the 2014 election both Morse and Giron's replacements lost to the Democrats. However, Hudak's replacement lost to a Republican, which in the end resulted in the Republicans taking control over the Senate, though, as we'll see ,the Republicans may have earned the wrong lessons from this recall effort.

2018 – California Josh Newman – Newman's recall is in some ways the mirror image of Denham. The recall was ostensibly about Newman's support for an increase in the gas tax and DMV fees. Newman also represented a critical vote in the legislature – he was the Senator that pushed the Democrats over the two-thirds in their control of the Senate. If he kept his seat, the Democrats, with supermajority support in both houses and control over the Governor's mansion, would be able to pass constitutional changes. The result was a recall campaign against the single most vulnerable Democrat. The Democrats in the legislature passed several bills (discussed below in the Newsom section) that would work to delay the recall effort. In a sense, they succeeded and the recall was scheduled concurrent with the 2018 primary day. However, they clearly didn't read the special elections vs. general election section. Newman was badly defeated, with 58% of the vote against him. His replacement was Ling Ling Chang, who Newman defeated in 2016. As already mentioned, Newman actually received almost 16,000 more votes in the recall portion than Chang did in her replacement race. But there's a big postscript: In 2020, we had Newman-Chang III: The Thrilla in Orange County, where Newman came out on top, winning with 51.3% of the vote.

Chapter 4: Gavin Newsom, the 2018 freakout and the Coronavirus pandemic

As of this writing, the California Governor Gavin Newsom recall vote is scheduled for September 14. The Newsom recall succeeded in getting on the ballot for general reasons that are somewhat similar to what we saw with both the Davis and Walker recalls; though in one critical factor – the make-up of the electorate – the Newsom recall is very different.

The major precipitating event for Newsom is the coronavirus pandemic and the ensuing efforts to combat its spread with shutdowns. Without the pandemic, and one specific legal decision, there is little chance that the recall would have gotten to the ballot. But that's not the beginning of the story. A look back at the political environment in 2017-2019 shows that recall threats were in the air – and that conservative groups have been priming the pump for recalls against state-level officials since their disastrous 2018 election. We must first look at the craze for recalls that came out of the 2018 election to provide a roadmap for why Newsom got to the ballot.

2018 Election and the Republican Recall Focus

Recall threats became the order of the day after the 2018 election – a political disaster for Republicans, especially in many of the states that have recalls.[252] Rather than examine the setback, and make changes for 2020, state-level Republicans started calling for recalls against the newly elected Democratic governors of California, Colorado, Nevada, New Jersey, Oregon and Washington as well as numerous Democratic state legislators. The Republican governor of Alaska, Mike Dunleavy, also faced an ongoing recall campaign, though that is a bit of a different story. Dunleavy would have been replaced by a Republican and Alaska's unique political culture involves more cross-party alliance building.[253] But for the rest of the states, including California, the recall threats were straightforwardly political, and the attempts effectively started on or before day one.

Unlike many past recall efforts, the GOP party leadership took front and center roles in these recalls. By contrast, in the few state level recalls that have taken place in US history, party leaders generally took a hands-off approach to recalls, especially in the early going. Why? Perhaps it is because losing would make the leaders look weak and susceptible to challenges. It may also be that party leaders wanted to maintain some level of comity between the parties.[254]

---

[252] In addition to losing control of the House, Republicans lost seven governorships, including in Michigan, Nevada and Wisconsin. Republicans actually did well in the Senate races (netting two seats and ousting four Democratic incumbents), but perhaps worth noting that the two seats the Democrats took back to limit their losses were in recall states of Arizona and Nevada, while only one of the seats Democrats lost was in a recall state (North Dakota).

[253] Alaska's recall is ongoing because the state has no time limit on the collection of signatures. However, it looks like the recall has stalled out. The big difference between Alaska and the other states is that if Governor Mike Dunleavy was removed, he would be replaced by his Lieutenant Governor, another Republican. So the politics were quite different.

[254] In the Senate, party leaders did not campaign against each other (one wonders if that may be more of a practical issue). However that policy ended in 2004, when Republicans went after Minority Leader Thomas Daschle (D) (SD). Senator Robert Byrd: "It used to be unheard of for Senate leaders to seek an active role against each other in campaigns." Richard Simon, "Senate Leader Frist to Campaign Against Daschle," *Los Angeles Times*, May 21, 2004. https://www.latimes.com/archives/la-xpm-2004-may-21-na-decorum21-story.html

From the point of view of a recall, making it a clear partisan issue could doom it, as the voters just endorsed that candidate in the first place. We've seen the results of what were perceived as clear political recalls in California with Machado in 1995 and Denham in 2008. This policy could reasonably lead to longer-term problems for the party in the state, as it appears they are focused on trying shortcuts rather than appealing to voters to give them a majority of the votes.

But in our brave new world, where the juicy red meat for a base that feels cheated with every lost election is the most important currency, recalls are a popular idea. Since the current iteration is a Republican-focused phenomenon, it also must be considered that party leaders do not want to be outflanked on their right and face complaints that they are weak.[255] The fact that it may both fail and have a longer-term negative impact for the party is ignored for the more pressing (to the leaders) intraparty threat. And in fact, all of the recent attempts by Republicans have failed – with varying degrees of negative repercussions for the party.

Colorado is arguably the most prominent example of the negative repercussions. Congressman Ken Buck used his campaign for Colorado GOP Party Chairman to specifically call for recalls against Governor Jared Polis and members of the legislature. Buck's acceptance speech saw him declare: "We need to teach them how to spell R-E-C-A-L-L."[256] Recall efforts have since been launched to no avail against Polis, the Secretary of State and numerous Senators, including the Majority Leader. This was started before the COVID pandemic. None got enough signatures. Unfortunately for Buck and the GOP, the Democrats decided that Math was a better course of study – as such Colorado has gone from a safe red state that voted Republican in all but two presidential elections from 1952-2004, to one that handed its votes to Democrats in the last four. Biden got 55% of the vote, the most by any candidate since Ronald Reagan, and the Democrats ousted Senator Cory Gardner.[257]

Nevada saw negative impacts as well. While petitions were taken out against Governor Steve Sisolak over a kitchen sink of issues,[258] the bigger issue was the recall effort against three state Senators, which was started in 2017. Nevada Lieutenant Governor Mark Hutchinson[259] (R) argued a litigation case for a recall against three Senators: Democrats Joyce Woodhouse and

---

[255] Since the recall is more of a Western phenomena, it may makes sense that Republicans are looking at it, as the party's real collapse has been in the West.

[256] *Colorado Pols*, "Ken Buck's "Spell R-E-C-A-L-L" Speech Bites Back Hard," September 16. 2019. https://www.coloradopols.com/diary/128160/ken-bucks-spell-r-e-c-a-l-l-speech-bites-back-hard

[257] Colorado should also be a cautionary tale for anyone looking to play around with the Electoral College allocation method. Some Democrats debated moving Colorado to a district-based system in 2004, though a court threw it out. Joshua Spivak, "Play By the Rules, Colorado," *USA Today*, October, 19, 2004. They'd look quite foolish today (Trump won 3 of the 7 districts).

[258] Despite months of discussion, petitioners had the misfortune of filing for the petition in February 2020. After only getting 15,897 (unverified) signatures in 45 days (they had 90 day), petitioners ended up asking for more time. Unlike in California, the court rejected this move. Riley Snyder, "Judge denies Siolak recall group's request for more time to gather signatures," *Nevada Independent*, May 15, 2020. https://thenevadaindependent.com/article/judge-denies-sisolak-recall-groups-request-for-more-time-to-gather-signatures. There were also four other recall attempts during the coronavirus pandemic.

[259] Riley Snyder, "Indy Explains: Why the Lieutenant Governor can argue state Senate recall case without ethical conflicts," *Nevada Independent*, February 17, 2018. One of the partners at Hutchison's firm is quoted as saying "We just never even considered this was close to the universe of potential problems."

Nicole Cannizzaro, and Republican-turned-Independent Patricia Fairly. A successful recall of all three would have been enough to flip the chamber to Republican control. Court challenges and questions about a signature removal or strike law led this fight to drag on until mid-2019. In the end, petitioners didn't get any of the recalls on the ballot, as the Supreme Court stepped in to rule that the petitioners did not get enough signatures (though the court did not end up ruling on the constitutionality of the signature strike provision).[260] While Nevada was a disaster for the Republicans in 2018 (when the recalls were at their peak of attention), the 2020 election was more of a mixed bag, but certainly nothing to brag about for the GOP.[261]

Oregon saw State GOP Chairman Bill Currier serve as lead petitioner in two of five efforts to recall Governor Kate Brown (D), who herself ascended to the position following the resignation of Governor John Kitzhaber under the threat of a recall. The first recall in 2019 was ostensibly over complaints about a climate bill, the second over the coronavirus pandemic shutdowns. Oregon's recall effort stood out, as the state does not have a replacement race nor does it have a Lieutenant Governor. The result is that a successful recall would ordinarily result in the Secretary of State taking the position. But that itself would have been a court fight. The previous Secretary of State died and Brown appointed a Republican successor, former House Speaker Beverly Clarno, who was 83 years old. According to one popular (and very possibly correct) theory, Clarno was not eligible to move to the governorship in case of a vacancy. Oregon law appears to disallow the replacement by an appointed official, which would have led to State Treasurer Tobias Read (D) taking the position (Clarno's office itself argued that Read was next in line).[262] The situation was easily resolved by the recall efforts' failure to get 280,050 signatures. The party-led petition claimed to have been a mere 10% short this first time and the claimed to have handed in 277,254[263] valid signatures the second time (after originally claiming to have handed in over 290,000[264]). Needless to say, any claim by petitioners of how many signatures were collected and not handed in should always be viewed extremely skeptically.

And California was treated to this too. Governor Gavin Newsom faced six recall attempts. Former candidates, including losers in Senate and Congressional primaries in 2018, took out petitions on immigration, capital punishment and other kitchen sink issues for a recall.[265] None of the other attempts had any traction.

---

[260] Riley Snyder, "Supreme Court decision ends Republican-backed attempts to recall state senators," *Nevada Independent*, April 19, 2019. https://thenevadaindependent.com/article/supreme-court-decision-ends-republican-backed-attempts-to-recall-state-senators

[261] Democrats won at the presidential level with almost the exact same percentage as in 2016; Congress saw no change (3-1 Democrats); The Democrats lost a State Senate seat and 3 assembly seats, not enough to change anything.

[262] Gary A. Warner, "How a 1971 fishing trip helped make Kate Brown Governor," *Bend Bulletin*, August 3, 2019 – dated January 31, 2020. Bend Bulletin https://www.bendbulletin.com/localstate/how-a-1971-fishing-trip-helped-make-kate-brown-governor/article_d13816fe-b16b-591c-9253-e039564907c7.html

[263] James Rosen, "Total Recall: Studies find recall elections increasing, with incumbents facing tough odds," *TLA.com/Sinclair National Correspondent*, September 2, 2020.

[264] Jacob Roberts, "'I think we're going to make it' Organizer of Kate Brown Recall Effort says," *KDRV.com*, August 2020. https://www.kdrv.com/content/news/Recall-Kate-Brown-campaign-notches-281k-signatures-party-leader-s-572230651.html

[265] California Secretary of State at https://www.sos.ca.gov/elections/recalls/complete-list-recall-attempts

It was the fifth attempt led by retired Yolo County Sheriff Sergeant Orrin Heatlie that worked. Tom Del Beccaro, the former Chairman of the California Republican Party, eventually served a director of RescueCalifornia.org which pushed the recall forward. This was the 55th petition taken out against a governor in California history, but in one critical way, it was unlike any othe

Coronavirus Recall and the peculiarities of California law:

What was different about the fifth recall and all the earlier 2019 recalls in other states was the political situation that surrounded the coronavirus pandemic. State and local officials, especially school board members, faced a good deal of the anger from the policy implications dealing with the COVID pandemic.

In 2020 alone, 87 recall attempts were started against officials over pandemic policies, 80 of them targeting officials who took steps to mitigate the spread of the virus. Only two got on the ballot in 2020, and another six got there for 2021[266], but this represented the first time in my decade of tracking recalls that one specific issue was the cause of so many recalls.

Fourteen governors throughout the country faced a recall threat, almost all over their shutdown policies. Even Republicans in Arizona and Idaho were targeted. Only Georgia's governor was targeted from the other side for not putting in place shutdown provisions. But why was Newson the only one to get enough signatures?

As noted above with Davis, California has the easiest signature requirement in the country to ge on the ballot. It also has a well-established signature gathering industry. And the Newsom recall eventually got some money behind it. But unlike with Davis, the turnout in Newsom's election 2018 was pretty good, so that didn't help the petitioners. But what did was the combination of a misstep by Newsom and a surprising court ruling. In a political blunder, Newsom went to the French Laundry restaurant in November for a party with a political advisor that seemingly violated at least the spirit of the state's lockdown rules (there were also complaints about sendir his children to in-person schooling, though that seemed to receive only a small bit of attention).[267]

While the French Laundry dinner was a public relations debacle, that was not the decisive facto Rather, another, more under-the-radar event in November was the real difference maker. Sacramento Superior Court Judge James Arguelles[268] ruled that petitioners would have an extra

---

[266] In general, these recalls have failed. Only two officials faced elections at least in part on pandemic issues – on opposite sides of the issue -- and both were removed: A School Board member in White Pine, Idaho who voted to support distance learning and the Mayor of Oregon City, who opposed masks and social distancing. Three other School Board members resigned after facing recall threats -- two in West Ada, Idaho and one in Appleton, Wisconsin. The Mayor of West Plains, Missouri will resign, though he stated the resignation has nothing to do wit the threatened recall. In addition, the Mayor of Auburn, California died in a plane crash while signatures were bein gathered. In March 2021, six Idaho officials survived recall votes over pandemic-related issues.

[267] Carla Marinucci, "French Laundry snafu reignites longshot Newsom recall drive," *Politico*, November 25, 202(https://www.politico.com/news/2020/11/25/french-laundry-newsom-recall-drive-440736

[268] Arguelles came under some fire as the attorney who represented the petitioners was a former law partner. As th say in the law, the so-called Chinese Wall to protect firms from client conflicts is well-named, as it stops nothing. The case was originally assigned to a different judge, but Arguelles was presiding over the initiative cases on the subject. So they combined them. Phil Willon, "Judge and attorney in pivotal Newsom recall lawsuit were former

120 days to gather signatures for the recall effort (as well as for the initiatives trying to get on the ballot). This gave Republicans a full 280 days of signature gathering, enough to finally put them over the top. The Secretary of State (Alex Padilla, who Newsom later selected to replace Kamala Harris as U.S. Senator) had previously filed no opposition to the extension requests for the two ballot initiatives. The judge allowed the signature extension for all of the matters. There is no official reason why there was no appeal (it may be because of support for one of the initiatives), though Democratic consultant Garry South suggested that "…it got lost in the shuffle."[269] Unlike in 2003, the fact that California could get enough signatures on the ballot to recall its Democratic governor seemed to be a surprise. But this view fails to appreciate the true state of play. Despite being a deep-blue state, California is not the Democratic monolith that many seem to believe. Donald Trump got six million votes in 2020 in California – the state was his top state by pure numbers. (There are also 5.3 million registered Republicans in the state). If petitioners could get less than 25% of those six million votes to sign, the recall would get to the ballot.

The extra time helped them pull it off. The petitioners handed in the last of their 2,117,730 signatures on March 17 and the Secretary of State announced that they got 1,719,943 valid signatures, well over the 1,495,709 needed. The signature failure rate was about 19%, very close to what it was in the Gray Davis recall (a little under 18%).[270] These were almost certainly the most signatures handed in for any recall, or perhaps any ballot measure, in US history. I believe it is more than double the amount needed to get a presidential candidate on the ballot in all fifty states.[271]

Cross it off -- Signature Removal/Signature Strike Law

But for Newsom, unlike for Davis, the number of signatures mattered. Specifically, that the petitioners got 224,235 signatures over the required number.

During the Senator Josh Newman[272] recall effort, Democrats passed laws that were designed to delay recall efforts. In Newman's case, there was a hope that delaying the recall long enough to schedule it on the same day as a regular primary would help the Democrats. Among the changes enacted included increased time for the clerks and the department of finance to report how much running would cost (30 business days + 10 more days) and the same time for the legislature to allocate money for the recall.

But a separate provision gave Newsom a "fight-fire-with-fire" chance to ward off the recall. The law gave a targeted official 30 business days to collect counter-signatures – getting people who

---

artners," *Los Angeles Times*, June 7, 2021. https://www.latimes.com/california/story/2021-06-07/judge-attorney-ewsom-recall-lawsuit-former-law-partners Arguelles' history was interesting, as he was appointed to the court by chwarzenegger and nominated to the federal bench by Trump in June 2020, though the nomination was never dvanced to a Senate vote.

Lara Korte, "'Lost in the shuffle.' Did Democrats miss a chance to block a Newsom recall election?" *Sacramento ee*, March 15, 2021. https://www.sacbee.com/news/politics-government/capitol-alert/article249843718.html

One of the stranger claims of the recall effort was that Democrats would start collecting fake signatures and hand ose in as well to taint the recall effort. This was either a bizarre conspiracy theory (that would have been self-feating for Newsom – some of the signatures could slip in) or a blame-shifting event in case the recall failed. I think the number is 880,000 signatures.

See the discussion on the Senate recalls. And how confusing is it for me that the two names are so similar? Yes, der, I have repeatedly said Newsom when I meant Newman. Hopefully I didn't do it here.

signed the original petition to remove their names. The only signatures that count are those that signed the petition in the first place. In Wisconsin, where the names were reportable, this may have been doable. But California does not allow the revelation of the signers.[273]

The idea of signature removal traces back to the early days of the recall, though in 1915, a court ruled that signature removals were not allowed under California law, a decision that seemed to have held for more than a century.[274] Other states have adopted the law -- Colorado, Georgia, Louisiana and Nevada have strike laws. Nevada's law became the source of a lawsuit following the recall effort against two Democrats and one former Republican state Senator. Democrats collected 2,000 removal signatures. As noted above, the courts got involved, but eventually Nevada's Supreme Court threw out the recall for other reasons and did not rule on the legality of the signature removal law.

For Newman, the strike law did not help, as less than 900 signatures requested removal. But a separate recall in 2017 showed its power. Petitioners handed in enough signatures to get a recall against Newport Beach Councilman Scott Peotter on the ballot – they needed 8445. Peotter's counter-campaign collected 205 withdrawal requests, just enough to get the recall tossed out (petitioners ended up with 8339).[275]

At one point, Newsom's supporters had suggested waging a signature removal campaign,[276] but with 224,235 needed, the effort was abandoned. In the end, only 43 signatures were removed.[277]

Cost of the Recall:

The one argument that every official facing a recall uses is that the recall is an inappropriate waste of money. Dianne Feinstein used this argument to brilliant effect in defeating the 1983 San Francisco recall against her.[278] Omaha, Nebraska Mayor Jim Suttle also campaigned hard on this issue, barely beating back the recall in 2011.[279] Newsom's recall effort seemed to be leaning into this approach.

After some stories that took the pro-recall campaign number of $81 million at face value (which is almost the same price as the 2003 election) the California Association of Clerks and Election

---

[273] Thereby minimizing the value of the personalized touch of hired goons. During the Newsom recall, Newman proposed a bill that would have given the targeted official a small ability to check names of signers, but the bill died on the vine, Let's see if it makes a comeback.

[274] Bird & Ryan, 327. *Laam v. McLaren*, 28 Cal. App. 632.

[275] Hillary Davis, "Effort to recall Newport Beach Councilman Scott Peotter fails," *LA Times/Daily Pilot*, December 12, 2017. https://www.latimes.com/socal/daily-pilot/news/tn-dpt-me-recall-fail-20171212-story.html

[276] One of the leaders of this short-lived effort was also a leader of the Denham recall effort -- Adrienne Moore, "Former State Senator Don Perata Leading New Campaign Against Gov. Newsom's Recall," *CBS Sacramento* April 6, 2021. https://sacramento.cbslocal.com/2021/04/06/former-state-senator-don-perata-leading-stop-the-stealnew-campaign-against-gov-newsoms-recall/

[277] Mychael Schnell "California secretary of state confirms Newsom recall election," *The Hill*, June 23, 21. https://thehill.com/homenews/state-watch/559994-california-secretary-of-state-confirms-newsom-recall-election

[278] Cronin, 140.

[279] Maggie O'Brien, "Suttle Recall backers want 30,000 names in 30 days," *World-Herald News Service*, October 21, 2010. https://nonpareilonline.com/archive/suttle-recall-backers-want-30-000-names-in-30-days/article_ee19c36d-3d93-5de5-b39d-56a554d9b245.html

Officials suggested a whopping $400 million price tag.[280] Eventually, the final number came down to $215 million.[281]

Check the Box! The Party Designation Fight:

In 2019, the legislature passed a law allowing recall targets to list their party designation on the ballot. However, the designation had to be filed with Newsom's official response to the recall – which was way back on February 28, 2020. Newsom failed to do so with his original response. After the recall actually got enough signatures, Newsom sued the Secretary of State (who he had appointed to the position).

Newsom lost this case, as Superior Court Judge James Arguelles (who granted the recall 120 extra days) ruled that Newsom did not hit the deadline to list the party affiliation. Newsom asked that the judge rule the failure to file the designation as a "good faith error" during Newsom's official response on February 28, 2020, but this was rejected due to the clear language of the statute. This was due to a new law that was approved and signed into law in October 2019. Prior to that, the recall had no party affiliation listed.[282] We'll see if it makes a difference.

The Campaign Finance issue

"There are two things that are important in politics. The first is money and I can't remember what the second one is' -- Mark Hanna, the political consultant GOAT.[283]

In a similar manner to Wisconsin, California treats a recall as two separate events: The yes or no vote on removing the elected official (i.e. the recall) is not considered a candidate election. Instead it is a ballot measure. The replacement race (in which the removed official is not allowed to run) is a candidate election.

This is no esoteric division. By virtue of the fact that it is a ballot measure, the official facing the recall can receive unlimited donations from each donor. The pro-recall campaign has the same advantage, but any of the potential replacement candidates have a limit of only $32,400 per donor, though there are ways of getting around this law with other organizations.

---

[280] Giacomo Luca, "This is how much it may cost to recall Governor Newsom," *ABC 10*, April 26. 2021. https://www.abc10.com/article/news/politics/newsom-recall-cost-california-governor/103-2f285ae0-3eda-4d43-b4f6-48e83ac43c70

[281] John Myers, "Democrats push for speedy Newsom recall as new analysis pegs cost at $215 million," *Los Angeles Times*, June 10, 2021. https://www.latimes.com/california/story/2021-06-10/newsom-recall-election-will-cost-taxpayers-215-million-officials-estimate

[282] Phil Willon, "Newsom won't be listed as a Democrat on recall ballot, judge says," *Los Angeles Times*, July 12, 2021. https://www.latimes.com/california/story/2021-07-12/newsom-wont-get-democrat-beside-his-name-on-recall-ballot-says-judge

[283] The second part of the quote has been presented in numerous different responses, but all mean the same. And, okay, we can make cases for James Madison and Martin Van Buren. But they were both presidents, and neither faced intra-party battles to get the nomination – and that's where the real challenges lies (winning the presidency itself is more a matter of being in the right year than the right candidate). Who else though?

So far, Newsom has taken full advantage of this law, raising over $51 million by August, with the biggest single donation from Netflix's CEO Reed Hastings, who gave $3 Million.[284]

The pro-recall effort has raised a fraction of that -- $6 million -- and most of the money went to getting the recall on the ballot. The Republican National Committee gave $250,000. However, the replacement candidates have raised many millions more than that, though still nowhere near what Newsom raised. Future pro-recall donations will go to the candidates themselves, who will be looking to distinguish themselves from each rather than to efforts to tear Newsom down.

We probably can expect this disparity to grow. Big money donors see an advantage in giving money to a sitting official, who is likely to stay in office and may not be too happy with any donors who placed the bet against him. The donors are also well aware that a Republican governor would be heavily constrained by the veto-proof majorities in the legislature. If you are looking to do business in the state, the best investment is in Newsom.

While some of the Republicans raised over $4 million and others are ultra-rich self-funders, the money is likely to remain a serious advantage for Newsom. Republicans also have to be concerned about people fundraising off the event and keeping the money for other uses, a problem they ran into with the Georgia Senate races.[285]

In the Walker recall, we saw some of these factors play out. Walker had a shorter time frame than Newsom to raise unlimited funds, but he ended up outspending his rival over 2-1 in by far the most expensive election in Wisconsin history.

Contra Hanna, money may not be everything – note the Michigan recalls in 1983, where the two Senators outspent their opponents 10-1 and still lost[286] – but it's hard to believe that it isn't a critically important advantage for Newsom.

Patience is a virtue -- Should the Democrats have delayed the recall vote?

With the polls showing Newsom in the lead, the Democrats took a fast track approach – or as Los Angeles Times' columnist Mark Barabak called it, "if you've got the votes, call the roll."[287] The legislatures passed A.152, which allowed them to waive the 30-day cost review process if the legislature approves funds for the recall (which they did). Republicans accused Democrats

---

[284] Seema Metha and Maloy Moore, "Newsom and his allies raise tens of millions more than recall backers and GOP candidates," *Los Angeles Times*, August 4, 2021.

[285] Rob Pyers from the California Target Book points out one potential candidate who never filed paperwork but kept fundraising as a GOP candidate. https://twitter.com/rpyers/status/1416961595171774467. On Georgia, see Shane Goldmacher and Rachel Shorey, "Trump's Sleigh of Hand: Shouting Fraud, Pocketing Donors' Cash for Future," *New York Times*, February 1, 2021.

[286] Braun, Total Recall.

[287] Mark Z. Barabak, "Why Newsom may prefer early California recall election vote," *Los Angeles Times*, June 1, 2021. https://www.latimes.com/politics/story/2021-06-01/gavin-newsom-early-california-recall-election-vote

d Newsom of "cheating" by taking a fast track approach.[288]

question the political wisdom of this fast track plan. "Calling the roll" meant scheduling an
ent at least two months in advance. While the desire to schedule the recall seems to be borne
it by a fear that something can go wrong or of giving the Republicans more time to rally around
single candidate who can catch fire, these both can easily happen in the shorter timeframe as
ell. The extra time doesn't add that much to the danger.

ewsom has the number advantage in California. What he needs is turnout. I would argue that
rnout is generally an overrated issue in American general election politics. When turnout goes
• for one side, there is frequently an effect on the other side, resulting in a boost in their
imbers. What Newsom sacrificed for the earlier date was different ways to goose the turnout
imbers:

More time to get away from any lingering complaints of the pandemic. The theory here may
• that the pandemic is less likely to impact closer to the summer than the fall. They did not
em to have counted on the Delta Variant.

Enough of a cushion to make sure that any problems with school reopening is worked out
fore the vote. This is one area that an "early surprise" can truly blow up in Newsom's face.

Money -- and lots of it. This extra money will allow Newsom to dominate the campaign and
e airwaves. The longer timeframe he has, the better that a strong campaign works.

As mentioned, in 2008, Michigan Speaker of the House Andy Dillon faced a recall vote. The
call was scheduled for November -- the same day as his re-election run. If Dillon was removed,
would only be out for a few months. Presumably, the two votes would be very similar. They
ere, but the discrepancy may mean something. Dillon won the recall vote 14,257-23,987, and
won his re-election race 14,311-27,864. Now you can say there is a natural drop off in vote as
gets further down the ballot. But that drop off is not evenly distributed. The kick-Dillon-out
mpaign lost only 54 votes. But the keep-Dillon-in-power saw a drop-off of 3,877. This is one
ce. Maybe you feel it's not so important. I would argue that what this may show is voters in
vor of the recall are more motivated and interested in punishing the elected official. Which
ings us to...

As discussed in the special election vs. general election section, one of the reasons recalls
em to work is that there is a "movers' advantage" to recalls. The voters who are most engaged
d most enraged are the ones in favor of the recall. We've seen polls suggesting that the pro-
call people are the ones most likely to turn out. More time will allow Newsom and the
emocrats to educate voters about the recall and make sure that they get out and cast their ballot.
ore time can help Newsom organize this turnout and education effort, which may be more
portant than any other factor in his survival.

Kathleen Ronayne, "GOP Says California Dems are 'cheating' in recall after state lawmakers pass bill aimed at
eding up election," *Associated Press,* June 28, 2021. https://ktla.com/news/california/gop-says-california-dems-
cheating-in-recall-after-state-lawmakers-pass-bill-aimed-at-speeding-up-election/

I'd say that a longer campaign would have been a risk worth taking for Newsom. Increasing turnout and leaning into your monetary advantage is likely to be more valuable than focusing on what the opponents can do.

Carnival of the Stars! Or Not.

In the early going, the recall effort seemed to be a reboot of the 2003 race, with a poorer cast of characters. There was an expectation that the number of potential candidates could equal or top the 135 in the 2003 recall, especially with the low barrier for entry and the potential for social media value for any candidate. But due to a mix of issues, including the requirement for tax disclosures, the belief that Newsom will win, and the fact that the race has not caught fire may have more discouraged more potential candidates. Only 46 candidates met the requirement to run in the recall, 21 of them were Republicans, nine were Democrats.

Candidates may have been inhibited from joining the race due to a new California law requiring anyone running to release their last five years of tax returns. The law was passed to force presidential candidates to submit their taxes to public viewing. The law was thrown out in relation to federal candidates, but still operates for state-level candidates in a primary. However, one candidate who was barred, challenged the rule and a judge decided that the tax disclosure law is not applicable to special elections like the recalls (and it seems there is no appeal). The law may have stopped a number of candidates, but the single candidate who challenged it, Larry Elder, did not have to submit his taxes or face any real negative repercussions for not doing so.[289]

The lion's share of early attention went to former Olympic Decathlon Champion Caitlyn Jenner, who is probably now best known as a reality TV star. Jenner's launch was treated as major news on conservative media. However, Jenner has had a rocky road, with repeated missteps, including an interview in her aircraft hangar where she focused on another plan owner moving out of state.[290] While Schwarzenegger was already political engaged before running for governor, Jenner seems to have rarely voted and actually left the campaign to film scenes for an Australian version of Big Brother. John Cox, the self-funding candidate who Newsom walloped in 2018, also jumped in, as have five separate Kevins (including the former Mayor of San Diego Kevin Faulconer and a leading Assemblyman, Kevin Kiley) and former Congressman Doug Ose. One of the few and seemingly best known Democrats, Kevin Paffrath, is an internet personality known as Meet Kevin.

Despite the attention paid to Jenner, the biggest names seemed to be Faulconer, who could boast that he was the last Republican in the country to lead a million+ population city and Kiley, who was a leading legislative opponent of Newsom and wrote a book calling for his recall. However, right before the filing deadline, conservative talk radio host Larry Elder jumped in the race and won his suit over the tax disclosure law. In retrospect, Elder's waiting appears to be very savvy. Elder's well-known presence in the conservative media world, and his jumping into the race

---

[289] Laurel Rosenhall, "Judge Puts Larry Elder on Recall Ballot, Throws Out Tax Return Requirement," CalMatters July 21, 2021. https://www.capradio.org/articles/2021/07/21/judge-puts-larry-elder-on-recall-ballot-throws-out-tax-return-requirement/

[290] Carla Marinucci, "Jenner has hangar pains after Hannity interview," *Politico*, May 6, 2021. https://www.politico.com/states/california/story/2021/05/06/jenner-has-hangar-pains-after-hannity-interview-1380759

when other candidates had either floundered or failed to gain traction, appeared to have immediately catapulted him into the top ranks of the replacement race. He did not spend money and credibility during the time period when voters were not focused on the recall, so he was still fresh and new when the recall suddenly came into public focus. He quickly raised over $4 million dollars and has led in many polls for the replacement candidates (albeit never topping 30% of the vote).

Elder's campaign is also paradoxically helped out by the fact that Newsom clearly sees treating Elder as the Republican candidate as a benefit to his campaign. It gives Newsom a solid candidate to attack and play "compare and contrast" with. Additionally, Elder has 30 years or more of inflammatory statements made on talk radio and other outlets. This provides Newsom with an overabundance of material for the campaign. For Elder, it gives him more press and credibility. The result is that the other candidates are crowded out.

The Democrats' Lesson from 2003: Win or Go Home

The focus of the Democrats has been to avoid having a prominent Democrat or liberal run for the position. The party was scarred by the 2003 run of Lieutenant Governor Cruz Bustamante, whose campaign slogan, "No on the Recall, Yes on Bustamante," helped no one. Bustamante served as a great cautionary tale for not only the party, but also for any candidate who wanted to run. Not only did Bustamante lose the recall, but in 2006, he ran and lost a run for state Insurance Commissioner. Along with Schwarzenegger's re-election victory in 2006, this represented the last time a Republican won a statewide office.

Over the months of the recall, a number of names were floated as potential candidates on the Democratic side, including billionaire and Democratic Presidential candidate Tom Steyer and former L.A. Mayor Antonio Villagrossa, who came in a third in the 2018 race (topped by Newsom and Cox). In the end, only nine people who cited their party affiliation as Democrats ran and none were current or former elected officials. Newsom has since adopted a strategy of "leave the replacement blank." This presumably allows Newsom to have a consistent message. If successful, say Newsom wins and blank performs strongly or wins the day, then it would help Newsom in 2022, as these candidates would be exposed as lacking in enough power to take on Newsom. In 2003, eight percent of ballots left the replacement candidate blank (4.6 percent of ballots left the recall portion blank).

The party has taken some heat for this "burn the boats" strategy, where there is no retreat to a safe candidate. However, it is likely the right move. A replacement candidate could have led voters who dislike Newsom an option to roll the dice and hope their candidate wins with a "yes on the recall, yes on Democratic replacement candidate." If there was a serious candidate, the Republicans are likely to have managed to consolidate support around one leading candidate. The reality is that Democrats are right in that a one-day, two-step recall is unlikely to elect a "safety" candidate.

Did Newsom cause a bump in recalls in 2021?

2021 has seen a boom in prominent recalls in California. In addition to Newsom, Los Angeles District Attorney George Gascon and San Francisco District Attorney Chesa Boudin are both facing recall efforts. Sonoma County District Attorney Jill Ravitch had her recall reach the ballot.

The San Francisco School Board is facing a high-profile recall effort as are Los Angeles Counci members and Shasta County Supervisors. The San Diego City Council President just saw a reca effort fail to get enough signatures. So I've been asked: Is the Newsom recall to blame?

I would say no. Some of these recalls are about the same issue, the coronavirus shutdowns.

We've seen recalls launched throughout the country on that subject. I see no reason to believe that the Newsom effort really fired it up.

Others are the garden variety recalls that would occur any year. In the NYT article, I note that California had 61 recall attempts in 2020, 11 went to a vote and 8 led to a removal. [291] It could b we are on a similar track this year as well. Perhaps the best way is examining the District Attorney recalls, which are the next prominent examples.

The District Attorney Recalls: LA's Gascon/SF's Boudin and others

District Attorneys are rarely targeted by recalls. [292] North Dakota's Attorney General lost a recall in 1921, but that was part and parcel of another fight entirely. There have been only seven recall attempts against California Attorneys General (and none have gotten to the ballot). Bird & Ryan note that the Kern County D.A. lost a recall vote in 1917, and the San Francisco D.A. survived one in the same year. The last notable one was in 2001, when the Marin County D.A. survived one launched by medical marijuana advocates (oh, how times have changed).

Over the last ten years, there has only been four recalls against elected attorney positions, with only one in California. San Bernardino City Attorney Jim Penman lost his seat in 2013, and that role is more of a defense attorney for the government.

Why are there few recalls of D.A.s? For one, there are fewer D.A.s. How many elected officials are in Los Angeles County? With 88 incorporated cities in the county, we can assume it is well into the hundreds. But only one of them is a District Attorney.

The other reality is that D.A.s, like judges, have historically been less able to upset large groups of constituents than legislative and executive positions like mayor and city council. They have instead been viewed as crusading defenders of the people. Usually, it would take a very prominent blown case or a corruption scandal to get negative attention for a D.A. at election time. [293]

---

[291] Jill Cowan, "Local Recalls, by the Numbers," *New York Times,* July 9, 2021. https://www.nytimes.com/2021/07/09/us/ca-recall-elections.html
[292] Joshua Spivak, "District Attorneys Get the Recall Spotlight: Why the Gascon and Boudin Recall Efforts Seem S Unusual," *Recorder,* March 23, 2021. https://www.law.com/therecorder/2021/03/23/district-attorneys-get-the-recall-spotlight-why-the-gascon-and-boudi recall-efforts-seem-so-unusual/
[293] "Only 25% of elected prosecutors nationwide faced an opponent for re-election and nearly half of candidates running for open seats ran unopposed." Scott Morris, "Alameda County District Attorney Nancy O'Malley is

However, progressive groups have led a nationwide push back against tough on crime prosecutors which has changed that equation. The breakthrough happened in 2017 in Philadelphia, with the election of former public defender Larry Krasner. Since then, we've seen a number of successful insurgent campaigns, frequently backed by George Soros, which has led to a different style of prosecutor. In California, both Gascon and Boudin are part of this trend.

The result has been a counterattack with recalls against these new, more liberal prosecutors. Pennsylvania legislators are looking to reverse the Supreme Court decision from 1978 and allow Philadelphia to have recalls, seemingly solely to target Krasner.[294] The recall efforts against Gascon and Boudin have been focused on their own policies, plus criticism of a perceived rise in crime in the two areas (Sonoma County D.A. recall is more of traditional one – it was launched by a disgruntled owner of senior care homes. This recall has actually gotten onto the ballot).[295]

Recalls against D.A.s are rare, but any radical change in policy is one way to bring about an effort. For a number of reasons, the Gascon recall is a real long shot. The amount of signatures needed to get Gascon on the ballot – over 579,062, more than was handed in for any office but the California Governor, is a huge mountain to climb. Additionally, in the election, Gascon, the former San Francisco District Attorney and Police Chief, received the support of high profile elected officials.

Boudin who has two recalls efforts against him (though the one led by a former Republican Mayoral candidate has failed, petitioners claim by 1714 signatures).[296] The fact that the signature total is so much less (51,325) improves the odds. Boudin, a former public defender, is a relative political outsider. He is simply an easier target. Still, the Boudin recall will be a tough road simply due to the sheer amount of signatures needed.

As a political topic takes the news by storm, it is not that surprising that it attracts recall efforts. We'll see if D.A.'s now become a regular target or if the fight fades into the background once the current political environment changes.

---

stepping aside," *Berkeleyside,* July 18, 2021 citing Carissa Bryne Hessick, "The Prosecutors and Politics Project: National Study of Prosecutor Elections," UNC February 2020. https://www.berkeleyside.org/2021/07/18/alameda-county-district-attorney-nancy-omalley-is-stepping-aside Hessick, https://law.unc.edu/wp-content/uploads/2020/01/National-Study-Prosecutor-Elections-2020.pdf
[294] The lead sponsor says it is not to target Krasner, but… c'mon. "Bill to let Philly voters recall elected officials gets vote," *Associated Press,* June 16, 2021. https://www.lockhaven.com/news/pa-news-apwire/2021/06/bill-to-let-philly-voters-recall-elected-officials-gets-vote/
[295] Emma Murphy, "Jill Ravitch supporters say recall is about one man's revenge," *Santa Rosa Press Democrat,* July 28, 2021. https://www.pressdemocrat.com/article/news/jill-ravitch-supporters-say-recall-is-about-one-mans-revenge/
[296] Joe Kikira, "Original Recall Chesa Boudin effort fails to get enough signatures," *SFist,* August 11, 2021 https://sfist.com/2021/08/11/original-recall-chesa-boudin-effort-fails-to-get-enough-signatures/

Chapter 5: Lessons Learned from Looking at the Recall in Action

In many ways, this is the most useful chapter – statistics and facts about the recall. But this certainly doesn't lend itself to a narrative or clear and easy to distill storylines. So instead we will proceed by topic.

Collecting the signatures:

The real challenge for recalls is not the election, but getting on the ballot. I would estimate that somewhere between two-thirds and three-quarters of recall attempts fail because petitioners cannot get the signatures. As we saw earlier, the signature requirements vary greatly, especially on the local level. There is always a debate about paying people to collect signatures, though most places allow it. It is actually an old idea, as Bird & Ryan note that the going rate used to be 10 cents a signature, with "Battle-scarred war veterans" and "indigent but deserving widows" serving as the best petitioners.[297]

But even if petitioners collect enough signatures, they have another big hurdle to overcome – getting the right signatures. Signatures will be tossed out. The reasons are all over the place, which is not a surprise, especially when you're asking random people on the street to sign, and frequently paying people to collect. Over nine years, I saw at least 129 recall attempts fail after enough signatures were tossed out to push the petition to below the needed signature requirement.

Among the frequent problems that crop up are signers who are not registered to vote, petitioners signing more than once or living out of district or state or even using a fake name.[298] Petitioners need to build a cushion. This cushion ranges widely – in Wisconsin, due to its "eligible voter" instead of "registered voter" requirement, the cushion may be less. In some places, we've seen 40 percent or more of signatures thrown out.

I've seen it suggested that the general rule of thumb is a 10-15 percent failure rate, though I'm not sure where that is from (and the article links are now dead). It could be that the number is taken from an actual law in California. For state level recalls, all of the signatures must be verified. But local recalls are quite different. For a recall where more than 500 signatures are submitted, the clerks are allowed to use a random sampling verification technique. Under this procedure, they take a sampling of the signatures, then they determine the number of valid signatures and then they extrapolate. If the valid signatures equal more than 110 percent of the minimum number required to get on the ballot, the recall succeeds. If it is below 90 percent, it

---

[297] Bird & Ryan, 171.

[298] Just a guess, but in terms of actual fraud, the most common is signature gatherers faking names to increase their own payment. Otherwise, fraud is a relative rarity, though we've seen it happen in Michigan. Melissa Hudson, "Edward Pinkney sentenced on election fraud charges," *ABC57*, December 15. 2014. https://www.abc57.com/news/edward-pinkney-sentenced-on-election-fraud-charges . Japan just had a particularly crazy example of this, when someone hired people to copy hundreds of thousands of signatures out of phone book (and easily got caught). "Source spills beans on recall bid against Aichi Governor," *The Ashai Shimbun*, April 18, 2021. https://www.asahi.com/ajw/articles/14332985

fails. If it is between 90-110 percent, then the clerk must verify each signature to see if they meet the minimum.

But for anyone gathering signatures, the 10 percent total is wrong. The Gavin Newsom recall saw about a 19 percent signature failure; Gray Davis, about 18 percent.[299] These rates were actually much better in other recalls, perhaps because a concerted effort was made by petitioners to check (and possibly cure) the signatures before submitting them. In 2018, the Senator Newman recall petitions failed at over 25 percent. The 2008 recall effort against State Senator Jeff Denham, saw a 41.5 percent signature failure rate.[300]

Another prominent 2018 recall, against Superior Court Judge Aaron Persky, required 58,634 signatures to get on the ballot. But the failure rate was over 28 percent.[301]

Initiatives in California show similar failures. The highest profile initiative of 2020 (Prop. 22) needed 623,212 signatures and had a 22.5 percent failure rate. Prop. 15, a constitutional amendment that needed 997,139, had a 25.4 percent failure. Both of those saw spending in the neighborhood of $6 million to get on the ballot.

The petitioners in the Scott Walker recall garnered an enormous cushion. They handed in 931,053 signatures and they only needed 540,000. At the end of the day, 900,938 were found valid (4,001 duplicates, 26,114 struck out by staff). This is a 3.2% failure rate. For Lieutenant Governor Rebecca Kleefisch (who appeared on a separate petition), the failure rate was 4%.

The Wisconsin verification also appeared to be different and I am unsure if the fact that Governor Scott Walker effectively conceded the success of the signature gathering portion eliminated the challenges.

In the four 2012 Wisconsin Senate races, the failure rate seemed to range from 7.8-12%. 2011 saw a range from 6-27.5%.

The other recalls during the decade show a big swing. In 2013 in Colorado, Senate President John Morse had a 37.5 percent invalidation rate, but the second recall, against Senator Angela Giron saw a miniscule 6% rejection, apparently due to a new program that allowed petitioners to check the signatures online. In 2011, Arizona Senate Majority Leader Russell Pearce had a 42% failure rate, while in Michigan, a state with a more vibrant recall culture, Representative Paul Scott only had a 9.4% failure rate.

Technological Changes as the driver of recalls:

Why do recalls seem so much more prevalent – at least on the state level? I think the single biggest possible driver is technology.

One of the odd claims in 2003 was the recall petitioners claimed that Davis ran a blocking effort by hiring all the od petition-gathering companies.

This verification was under the random sampling technique (the law was changed in 2018 to remove state level alls, at least partially to slow the Newman recall effort).

The Persky recall was under the sampling technique.

If the problem in getting a recall to work is organizing and collecting signatures, then the technological revolution may have helped solve this. The internet, email and social media allow unconnected voters to be alerted, angered and drawn into a brewing battle; creating and sharing lists of likely signers is easier than ever, thanks to that first killer app, the spreadsheet.

Demographic data is now easily available to compile and parse online. Smartphones help organize signature gathering efforts. And campaigns are cheaper and easier thanks to the ubiquity of personal printers. In the Newsom race, having people print up the petitions greatly simplified the effort.

Fundraising has gotten much easier as well. The ability to easily collect small money donations have become through targeted emails and ads have reshaped lower level politics. My favorite example is the South Carolina Congressman, Joe Wilson, who yelled "you lie" at President Barack Obama's joint sessions Congress in 2009. Without any effort, and in a relatively non-competitive seat, he raised $1.8 million in a week, and his opponent got $1.6 Million.

This last election saw Democratic donors pour $100 million into the South Carolina Senate race and nearly as much into Kentucky. Both races turned out to be easy wins for the Republican incumbents.

The recall operates on the same principle, though it may take place more on the local level. But small money donations can easily flood in.

One ancillary part of this is something we are seeing in the Newsom recall. Some of the campaigns seem to be run solely to raise funds and perhaps siphon them to other causes.

The reality is that technology perhaps more than anything else, will help fuel future recalls.

Disorder in the House: Flipping the Chamber

Remember when we said that State Legislative Recalls are unusual because they are a strike against a political party? Well, here's some evidence the other way. Voters are very willing to cast a vote that will result in a switch in control of a legislative chamber.

We saw this happen in:

2012 in Wisconsin,
1996 in Wisconsin,
1995 in California (twice!)
1983 in Michigan

In the 2011-2012 recalls in Wisconsin and the recall in Washington in 1981, voters refused to recall Senators that would have led to a switch in control (though the Washington one was due a switch in parties, that led to a switch in control). Additionally, in 2018 in California, the recal

d to the Democrats losing their supermajority and if there was no resignation in the third olorado seat in 2013, we may have seen another flip. So:
lose margin in the legislature + very tight district + right issue = roll the dice on the recall.

ou have selected Regicide: Legislative leaders'edition302

ix times voters have been asked to kick out of office the leader of the legislature. Again, voters ave not been shy about making that big decision. In 2013 in Colorado, 2011 in Arizona and in)95 in California (again, Doris Allen is a very questionable example), voters gave up on their strict having the most powerful member of the chamber in order to punish the elect official. n the other hand, three officials have survived and none of these races were particularly close:)12 Wisconsin, 2008 in Michigan and 1994 in California.

urn Out – Should we actually expect it to go up?:

here is a widespread belief that one of the advantages of launching a recall for petitioners is that rnout drops, especially if it is held in an off-year or on a special election date. Turnout in US ections are always a moving target, but presidential election turnout is invariably vastly higher an in a midterm election, which itself is higher than in an off-year. There is a strong logic to e argument that you would expect lower turnout in a special election. Voters have to know)out the vote and care enough to show up for just one office. But the numbers don't tell this ory. On the local level, recall turnout can be all over the place. For state legislative recalls, the 'op-off theory seems to hold. Without going into all the numbers, we regularly see lower rnout in the legislative recalls than occur in the general election.

ut the theory is blown up when looking at the three gubernatorial recalls in US history. It is :actly the opposite. While Newsom may very well be different, the earlier examples show rnout shooting up.

1e Davis recall, held in October in an off-year, saw a massive voter boost. In 2002 for Davis' ection, only 7.7 million people voted. But they came out in force for the circus-like atmosphere the Davis recall, with 9.4 million votes cast. Looking ahead at Schwarzenegger's re-election ce in 2006, we see just how impressive the recall numbers were. Turnout for that race saw)ter interest drop, with 8.6 million coming to the polls.

Outside of the Simpsons reference, the Regicide/legislative leader comparison is from John Barry "The Ambition d the Power: The Fall of Jim Wright: A True Story of Washington; Viking Press, 1989. By now, Barry is super-nous and certainly doesn't need my help, but this book should be required reading to understand the "how we got re" in contemporary American politics. I would say there is no definitive book of the late 80s/early 90s period or ılly of what we can think of as the Republican Ascendency from 1968-1992 (Maybe Kevin Phillips' The nerging Republican Majority). The one book I've seen cited as the best of the era is Richard Cramer's What It kes, his episodic take on the 1988 presidential election. It's alright, but in terms of its relevance, you might as 'll be reading about the Cleveland v. Harrison. Cramer completely whiffs on the two big trends of that election – ise Jackson and the rise of African-American voting bloc in internal Democratic politics and, arguably more portant, Pat Robertson and the growth of the Christian Conservative right (I also absolutely don't buy that the cted officials are so disconnected from their campaigns, but whatever). Barry isn't dealing with that subject, but shows in real time the death of the old order and (in the persona of Newt Gingrich), what's coming next and how /ill engulf the political world.

The Walker recall in Wisconsin took place in an election year, but it was on a special election date in June. There was every reason to think the votes wouldn't be that impressive. In 2010, Walker won election with 2.1 million votes. But, 2.5 million came out in the recall. The number dropped back down in 2014, with 2.4 million votes.

The Frazier recall in 1921 in North Dakota, our third example, is a bit different. Frazier had a two year term, so his original election was in the higher-turnout presidential election year. Frazier won re-election with 229,606 voters. We can't fully use the numbers in his previous election in 1918 (because it took place before Women's suffrage) though that year saw only 91,250 voters. The 1921 recall saw 218,757 voters come out, which is a very small drop off from the 1920 election. The real comparison should be 1922 -- where turnout dropped to 191,469. In the other, high-profile recalls of executives (big-city mayors), we see strong turnout numbers as well. The 1983 recall of Diane Feinstein in San Francisco saw turnout higher for the April recall than the November re-election. In 2011, Miami-Dade Mayor Carlos Alvarez was kicked out, with more votes coming out for the recall than the 2008 election, and the results were simila for Omaha, Nebraska Mayor Jim Suttle, who survived a recall in 2011.

One unknown factor in the recall is that mail-in ballots will be sent to everyone. Colorado has a similar law, which did not help the two Senators in 2013 survive their vote, but it is really unclear what the impact of the mail-in ballot will be. Presumably, Newsom's forces believe it will help, as higher turnout in a very Democratic state should help him and, at the moment, the Republican Party has shifted against absentee voting.

Party Line -- Is one party more likely to use recalls?:

I constantly get asked about the party breakdowns of the recall. Most of the recalls are on the local level, where the position is elected on a nonpartisan basis. When there is a partisan position in local elections, the party label is frequently a misleading method to judge recall use, as many are not based on D v. R partisan motivations. The reality is that in America, most localities are one-party controlled areas.[303] The fight is over actual policy issues or it is intraparty.[304]

On the state level, we do see both parties (or, more accurately, supporters in both parties, not the party leaders themselves) using the recall, with the party's switching off in who is more likely to push for a recall effort. Of the 14 state legislative recalls from 1981-2008, most officials targeted were Democrats or people who were seen as supporting the Democrats.

In 2011-2012, Republicans were targeted in 14 recalls that got to the ballot, while Democrats were hit in only 4. Since then, it has been four Democrats who have been the focus of recalls. Outside of very tactical recalls (Denham in 2008, the counter-recalls against Democrats in 2011 or the ones over corruption (the two Oregon recalls, the one in Wisconsin in 2003), the recalls since 1971 have been against officials who were in the majority party in control of the legislatur

---

[303] Not all, and there are interparty recalls, but they are by far a minority.
[304] I'm sure others have noted this, but let me give the late, great Professor Ari Hoogenboom, master of the history of Rutherford B. Hayes, the credit as he explained about the Gilded Age that intraparty conflicts are by far the mos vicious because the policy differences are small, so this is a true fight over who gets to rule.

or (obviously) the gubernatorial mansion. Note the recalls targeting Republicans (in three different states in 2011) occurred right after the Democrats were walloped in 2010. So, which party is most likely to launch a recall? Simple -- the one that is not in power.

Second verse, same as the first? Recall Reruns are not uncommon

One of the replacement candidates in the Newsom race is John Cox, who Newsom beat in 2018. The losing Democratic candidate in 2012 to Scott Walker? Milwaukee Mayor Tom Barrett, who lost to Walker in 2010. Bill Simon, the Republican nominee in 2002 who lost to Gray Davis, made a run in the replacement race in the 2003 recall. Simon dropped out, but still came in 12th in the replacement race (with 8913 votes).

While most recalls are not reruns of the past election, there are more than enough of these rematches to show that candidates are very happy to try and relitigate their race. Two of the Wisconsin recalls were rematches, and one was a rerun of an Assembly race. The Newman recall in 2018 was not a straight rerun (as California has the two-step process), but the winner was the previous Senator, who lost to Newman in 2016 (and then went on to lose to Newman in 2020). The early controversial recall in 1914 of E.E. Grant also saw a rerun.

There may be a few reasons for the lack of rematches. It is not that losing candidates are chastised – many losers pull an Adlai Stevenson or Grover Cleveland and run again. It is also not because voters don't want to legitimatize a "naked power grab." As we've seen, voters have been willing to endorse a strictly political recall that is run simply to benefit one party.

The biggest problem is probably that the candidate may appear to be a sore loser who is trying to reverse, at the public's expense, a legitimate election vote against him/her. It can easily be seen as, or more likely turned into by the incumbent's judicious campaigning, a personal vendetta. On this same front, the opposition research has already been done, and the incumbent already knows the dirt to use.

Another powerful disincentive is that voters may see it as hijacking the voter anger (and the volunteer efforts, if any) of the recall for personal gain. While not a rerun, it's worth considering the efforts of Congressman Darrell Issa, who put in the money for the Davis recall, but dropped out of the race when other, more popular, candidates entered.

It also gives the incumbent someone to hit and run a race against. The recall suddenly becomes a straightforward political race – it is no longer just about voter anger or a diffuse electorate. The elected official can present ads against the alternative.

Reruns and rematches happen, especially on the local level. But they don't happen often enough to feel that they are a regular feature of the recall.

Blowouts v. Barnburners:

Many recalls are blowouts – one way or the other. Look at the three California recalls in 1995 to see this in play. But, for anyone interested in the Newsom race, there is an interesting dynamic in the gubernatorial recalls. All closely track the last election.

Frazier saw a 2% reversal. Davis went down 3%. And Walker went up a little less than 1%. This may mean that we shouldn't necessarily expect too much of a swing in any big recall.

Interest Group Failures in using the recall

Interest Groups have been remarkably successful in using the initiative. But does it works as well for recalls? Do voters care if the recall is perceived to be instigated by an interest group? Voters don't seem to object to political party backed recalls, but they seem less interested if the recall is clearly tied to a specific interest group. While there are plenty of counter-examples,[305] I think that voters are more likely to spurn the effort.

The unions may be the best example of this rejection. The 2011-2012 recalls were very closely tied to organized labor. One would be hard pressed to call these recalls a success. Beyond the fact that most of the targets survived, the union movement could not even successfully choose Walker's challenger. The unions backed Kathleen Falk, who finished 24 percentage points behind Thomas Barrett in the Democratic nomination fight. Interestingly enough the first state official to survive a recall vote (James Owens in California in 1913), faced the recall because of union efforts. Of course, our first ever recall, which resulted in the ouster of LA Councilman James Davenport in 1904, was pushed by unions.

Judicial Rulings and the Recall:

Over the years, state courts have spanned the spectrum in their rulings on recall laws. Courts have thrown out recall laws entirely, sometimes on extremely suspicious logic. Courts have also worked to defend and expand them. All the decisions cited are in State Court. As can be seen earlier, Federal Courts have been relatively quiet on recalls. These are some of the notable cases,[306] but there are many others to examine.

Anti-Recall Rulings:

The first important recall ruling seems to have been in 1912, when the Arkansas Supreme Court wiped out its recall law. Arkansas voters adopted an initiative law in 1911. In 1912, the first year that voters could propose measures, nine were brought before the voters. Only three of them passed, one of which was a recall law, which passed with 55% of the vote in favor. But the State Supreme Court quickly quashed it, holding that the 1874 Constitution limited three Constitutional Amendment changes in one term,[307] though a separate article suggests that it was rejected because it needed to receive a "Constitutional Majority" – a majority of total votes cast

---

[305] Arguably the 1990 in Wisconsin and 1994 in California recalls were both interest group based. The 2013 recalls in Colorado could be an example of officials losing in an interest-group (gun groups – though originally not the NRA) recall,

[306] I should point out right here that I have no access to Westlaw or Lexis and haven't for quite a long time. Therefore, my ability to search cases and contemporary law review articles is very limited. Needless to say, whatever bluebooking skills/knowledge I once had are long gone. I don't care and neither should you.

[307] *State ex. rel. City of Little Rock v. Donaghey*, 106 Ark. 56 (1912)

in the election instead of just on the specific issue.[308] As mentioned earlier, in 1932, Arkansas voters rejected an initiative that expanded terms and also included a recall provision. The three vote limit has prevented Arkansas voters from considering a recall law in recent years.

Pennsylvania:

In 1976, Pennsylvania's Supreme Court declared Philadelphia's recall law unconstitutional[309] in what Professor Jefferson Fordham called "one of the most extraordinary decisions of recent memory."[310] The court threw out a large number of signatures based on a very expansive view of who is allowed to notarize the petitions. In the view of Professor Fordham, the court "simply ignored the home rule concept and the constitutional provisions on home rule."[311] Georgia's Supreme Court limited the recall law, moving from a political recall to a Malfeasance Standard one. Georgia overwhelmingly passed a recall law in 1978, with 68% in favor. But a Georgia Supreme Court decision in 1988[312] invalidated the political recall code that the state legislature wrote to enact the law, with the justices ruling that the phrase "grounds" in the constitutional amendment meant that the law was a limitation on the use of the recall akin to a malfeasance standard. Two justices, including the Chief Justice, dissented. The dissent took a vastly more expansive view of the law, one that tracks the recall laws of political recall states, noting that "grounds" were "the vote of majority of electors in a recall election…"

Michigan:

In 1926, Michigan's Supreme Court held that the recall required a Malfeasance standard before the recall could proceed, which apparently prevented the recall from being used in almost all circumstances.[313] But a 1960 decision reversed the ruling and adopted the Political recall standard.[314]

Nevada:

In 2017, the Nevada Supreme Court ruled 4-2 that judges are not subject to the state's recall law.[315] Both the ruling and the dissent hold that judges are "public officers" as provided for in the recall law, but the majority ruled that the recall law was superseded by the 1976 creation of the Nevada Commission on Judicial Discipline. According to the majority, the fact that the act creating the Commission didn't specifically mention recalls removed the recall as an option for

---

[8] Calvin R. Ledbetter, Jr. "Adoption of Initiative and Referendum in Arkansas: The Roles of George W. Donaghey and William Jennings Bryan," *The Arkansas Historical Quarterly*, Vol. 51, No. 3 (1992) 199-223, 200, 221. The "Constitutional Majority" decision was in *Hildreth v. Taylor*, 117, Ark. 465 (1915).

[9] *Citizens Committee to Recall Rizzo v. The Board of Elections of the City and County of Philadelphia*, 47 Pa. 1 (1976)

"Jefferson R. Fordham, "Judicial Nullification of Democratic Political Process – The Rizzo Recall Case," *University of Pennsylvania Law Review*, November 1977, 1-18, 1.
https://scholarship.law.upenn.edu/cgi/viewcontent.cgi?article=4884&context=penn_law_review
Fordham, 12.
Mitchell v. Wilkerson, 258. Ga. 608 (1988) https://law.justia.com/cases/georgia/supreme-court/1988/45899-.html
Newberg v. Donnelly, 209 N.W. 572 (Mich. 1926), also Hanselman, 2014.
Wallace v. Tripp, 358 Mich. 668 (Mich. 1960).
Ramsey v. City of North Las Vegas, 392 P.3d 614, April 13, 2017.

future judges.

The majority ruling feels like a very tortured way to protect judges from the recall -- one that other states don't follow. Allowing for impeachment or removal by a commission is very common -- it is odd and extremely unlikely that voters were voting to remove the recall at the same time that they were putting forth another method of removing judges.

The behavior of the court in this case was highly suspect (though contemporary news coverage ignored it). The Supreme Court issued this ruling after an incredibly long delay, one that allowed any voter anger to completely dissipate by the time the ruling was handed down. The recall was brought against North Las Vegas Municipal Judge Catherine Ramsey in 2015. The Supreme Court took the case in July 2015, and heard oral arguments in October 2015. In that time, Ramsey admitted to misconduct. She was barred from seeking re-election (she tried to run for another seat), suspended, required to write apologies, and take a fitness test and the city eliminated the judgeship. Does the Nevada Supreme Court normally take a year and a half to rule on election law cases or was this more of a dodge?

This was not the only anti-recall ruling from the Nevada Supreme Court. A unanimous 2010 decision ruled that signers to the recall petitions had to be people who actually voted in the last election – registered voters were not enough. This decision invalidated a 2009 Nevada law that specified that any registered voter could sign. In a comment to a post on my blog, Richard Winger of Ballot Access News noted that this provision would likely violate US law from Bush v. Gore, which could make it susceptible to a challenging lawsuit.

Texas:

In El Paso, Texas, the Texas Eighth Circuit Court of Appeals threw out the recall against Mayor John Cook[316] and held that the recall proponents (most prominently Pastor Tom Brown and the World of Life Church) were on the hook for the $250,000 that Cook had spent fighting the recall. This unanimous decision held that the church was a corporation, and as such could not make an expenditure to a recall election (it needed to use a special purpose committee). What was unusual was that the court decided this was reason enough to throw out the signatures and rule that the election cannot take place. It is unusual that a recall would be tossed out based on violations of campaign finance laws rather than any issue with the recall itself. The decision also includes a serious bench slap of the trial judge for an "abuse of discretion" in not stopping the recall, saying that he failed to apply the law to the facts, "hindered the judicial process" and noted that the court should "...not be swayed by public clamor or fear of criticism." And this was for not stopping the election.

Washington State:

Washington State has apparently had quite a history with recall decisions, moving back and forth between a Malfeasance Standard and a quasi-Political Recall law. Joshua Osborne-Klein notes that "For a brief period in the 1960s and early 1970s, there was a trend to liberally construe the

---

[316] *City of El Paso v. Tom Brown Ministries*, Court of Appeals, Eighth District of Texas, No. 08-16-00075-CV
https://law.justia.com/cases/texas/eighth-court-of-appeals/2016/08-16-00075-cv.html

constitutional standards for recall by equating 'malfeasance' with any wrongful act."[317] This sentence would explain why the Senator Peter Von Reichbauer recall of 1981 was able to make it to the ballot. A 1984 decision seems to have settled the law permanently in favor of a Malfeasance Standard, though the dissent concludes that the "majority drastically changes the law pertaining to the right of recall. It admits as much when it states that it is overruling four prior cases."[318]

Noted Pro-Recall Rulings:

On the other side of the aisle, in 2011, Arizona's Supreme Court took a very strong stand in favor of an expansive view of the recall law. State Senator Russell Pearce tried to have the petitions against him thrown out due to minor technical deficiencies. He asked for a strict compliance standard for recall petitions. The court rejected this,[319] noting the fight over their constitutional ratification with Taft in 1911, and ruled in favor of a more liberal substantial compliance standard. The court noted that changing the standard "would fail to respect Arizona's strong devotion to recall as a progressive process intended 'for the benefit of the public rather than the officials.'... The delegates to the Constitutional Convention of 1910 were willing to risk statehood over a robust recall system that subjected every official to removal. Adopting a standard that makes it more difficult for the public to remove its own offices would frustrate this historical intent."[320]

Michigan:

Also in 2011, Michigan's Supreme Court threw out an appellate court ruling to stop the recall against State Representative Paul Scott. This ruling didn't seem to take any major steps in recall law.

Alaska:

In a 2021 ruling in the recall effort against Alaska Governor Mike Dunleavy (R),[321] the Supreme Court may have effectively overturned the malfeasance standard.

The ruling walks through Alaska's adoption of the recall law. The Constitution's delegates left it up to the legislature to draft laws setting up the recall provision. The legislators codified the law in 1960 and in 1972 prescribed the grounds and procedures for recall of local officials looking at the big court decision in 1984 that set Alaska on a "middle ground."

The 1984 Alaska Supreme Court ruling in Meiners v. Bering Strait School District held that the

---

[7] Joshua Osborne-Klein, "Electoral Recall in Washington State and California: California Needs Stricter Standards Protect Elected Officials from Harassment," *Seattle University Law Review*, 145-172. 167-168
https://digitalcommons.law.seattleu.edu/cgi/viewcontent.cgi?article=1804&context=sulr
Cole v. Webster, 103 Wn.2d 280 (1984), 291-292.
Ross v. Bennett, Arizona Supreme Court No. CV-11-0264-T/AP
https://www.azcourts.gov/Portals/0/OpinionFiles/Supreme/2011/CV-11-0264-143917.pdf
Ross v. Bennett, 10.
State of Alaska v. Recall Dunleavy, Supreme Court No. S-17706, No. 7542, July 16, 2021
https://cases.justia.com/alaska/supreme-court/2021-s-17706.pdf

recall law "should be liberally construed so that the people are permitted to vote and express their will" – though it was limited to the local level. On the state level, the liberal construction was not used, and recalls were rejected against a governor, two state senators and one assembly representative due to a failure to state a valid cause of action. This liberal construction decision could change that.

The decision doesn't spell out the potential impact, but both the partial dissent and the governor's statement do. The Governor's Statement:

"The Alaska Supreme Court today issued an opinion that creates a standardless recall process, subjecting elected officials at every level, and across the political spectrum, to baseless, expensive, and distracting recall elections by their political opponents."

From Judge Stowers' partial dissent:

"I urge every legislator to carefully consider the court's opinion today. The opinion opens the door to standardless recall petitions...The greatly expanded access to recall created by the court's decision today can and will be used not to actually seek to recall an elected official for cause, but instead to seek to recall an elected official because of disagreements over policy. And in Alaska, disagreement over policy or political philosophy is not a proper subject for recall.

Local Recalls:

In a perfect world, this book would be looking at every recall in US history. At the very least, I would be providing analysis of the local recalls that have taken place throughout the country since Los Angeles Councilman James Davenport was ousted in 1904. But that will have to wait for another day. Yet, I do want to touch on some of the local recalls without getting bogged down in minutiae.

With local recalls, we see attempts to stop them by refusing to schedule a recall. Most of the time these efforts fail, but at the very least they delay the recall and force recall proponents to spend money fighting the battle of getting the recall to be scheduled.

Another challenging situation that occurs with local recalls is when enough people are removed that the body (such as a city council) cannot form a quorum to vote and pay bills.

There are no comprehensive stats for recalls in the US, but over a decade I counted nearly a 100 recalls taking place in the US. A study in the 1970s saw similar totals, which leads to the question of how many recalls have taken place in the US. I imagine for many years it was quite bit less than 1000 per decade (simply because there were fewer states that had recalls). This is borne out by the Bird & Ryan numbers, which suggests only 155 recalls in California's first 26 years of the device led to a vote or resignation. So I would guess in the 117 years since Davenport was kicked out, there were probably between 7,000-10,000 recall elections that got t the ballot. Of those, 99% were on the local level.

There is no commonality between these recalls. Over this decade, the only year that there were a large number of recalls dealing with a single national question was 2020 over the Coronavirus pandemic. But even there, only two got to the ballot in the calendar year (and perhaps 10-20 in 2021).

If there's one issue that seems to be the most likely to lead to someone facing a recall is that official having fired an appointed official, like a City Manager or a Police Chief. Other prominent recall subjects are development policies, taxes, combining schools, record-keeping and a failure to hold open meetings (which is popular in the Malfeasance Standard states). But many times we get…different issues. Let's look at some of those:

The recall's finest hours: Battling KKK

While still disturbing, the KKK is today only a fringe group in American politics. Not so in the 1920s.[322] The KKK was a major political force in America, causing untold damage to the country. The recall was actually used to combat this nefarious presence. In their contemporaneous account, Bird & Ryan note: "An explanation of the unusual recall activity of recent years may be found largely in the malevolent buffoonery of the Ku Klux Klan, the growing pains of mushroom cities, and the desire of deposed political factions for reprisal."[323] In 1924, "Klan pestilence descended on Anaheim with all the barbarous buffoonery that was characterizing its visitations of thousands of American towns and cities…" All non-Klan members of the police force were fired, confirming that "the city was under the sway of a 'Klan Controlled 'Kouncil.'" In the fight that followed, four of five city councilmembers, all KKK members were tossed out in February, 1925. A counter-recall launched against the fifth (anti-Klan) councilman failed. Turnout was 93%.[324]

Bird & Ryan also note a number of other KKK focused recalls: an Azusa Trustee removed because of a "certain indulgent attitude on Mr. Beck's part toward matters not approved by the local organization of the Ku Klux Klan.";[325] A Kern County Justice of the Peace kicked out when "the public apparently was passing judgment on Cook as a Klansman rather than on Cook as a judge."; as well as recalls against a Kern Supervisor and an official in Riverside. On the other side of this coin, a Covina Mayor was kicked out in 1926 with the support of "narrow religious interests affiliated with the Klan."[326]

---

[22] This 1920s version of the KKK is different than the original post-Civil War version, which was focused on terrorizing and murdering the newly freedmen in the South. Open question: Does Amos Akerman's prosecution of the KKK make him the greatest Attorney General in US history? The 1920s version was a national movement and, in addition to murdering Blacks, also focused on terrorizing immigrants in the country. An example of cognitive dissonance in politics is that the KKK had success in the Democratic Party, which that same decade, nominated a Catholic to run as President. Part of the reason for the lack of attention to the political dynamic is that there is little in the way of movies/books on this part of the story. Boardwalk Empire is one of the few shows or movies that deal with the growth of the KKK in that decade.

[23] Bird & Ryan, 345.

[24] Bird & Ryan, 136-140.

[25] Bird & Ryan, 130-131.

[26] Bird & Ryan, 296. There is also an official in Lynwood, though that one seems to be a little less clear.

KKK recalls may have taken place throughout the country, but I have only seen one – perhaps the most prominent of them -- and one that came back into the news recently.
Denver, Colorado Mayor Benjamin Stapleton was a member of the KKK, winning election in 1923 by denying this. However, after numerous appointments of KKK members, petitioners got a recall on the ballot. In order to survive, Stapleton pledged to "work with the Klan and for the Klan in the coming election, heart and soul," and said he'd "give the Klan the kind of administration it wants" – including appointing a KKK member as Police Chief. In 1924, Stapleton won the recall race, which was a re-run against former Mayor Dewey Bailey. Stapleton broke with the Klan in 1925. Last year, the neighborhood of Stapleton changed its name to remove the honor.

Segregation recalls:

Southern states have not been a major player in recalls, but they had a major recall in the Civil Rights Era. Little Rock's public high schools were all closed to stop desegregation in the so-called "Lost Year" when Little Rock's public high schools were all closed in a failed attempted to stop desegregation (though high school football was apparently allowed to continue).

Following the white supremacists' attempted "purge" of 44 teachers and principals, recall efforts were organized against both sides. Three segregationist members of the board were voted out on May 25, 1959, dealing a fatal blow to Governor Orville Faubus' segregationist efforts.[327]
On the other side of the fight for Civil Rights, in 1963, six city council members were kicked out of office in Statesville, North Carolina (at the time, it was called the City of Progress) over their votes to integrate the city's two swimming pools.[328]

The Big Cities:

Probably the most notable recall effort against a local official was San Francisco Mayor Diane Feinstein, who beat a recall vote with 81% in her favor in 1983, using the argument that the device should not be used for simple policy disagreements and that her recall was a waste of money.[329] Feinstein's recall was over gun control, as a far left group called the White Panthers launched the recall. Feinstein saw an opportunity and, as mentioned below, easily defeated the recall and used it as a way to set herself up on the path to national power.

In Los Angeles, the largest municipality in the country to have the recall, four mayors have faced recall elections, and two were removed, the previously noted A.C. Harper and Mayor

---

[327] H.M. Alexander, The Little Rock Recall Election, New York, McGraw-hill, 1960.
[328] Mike Cline, "When Velma took a stand: Statesville voters ousted council when it tried to integrate public pools," *Salisbury Post,* February 6. 2017. https://www.salisburypost.com/2017/02/06/velma-took-stand-statesville-voters-ousted-council-tried-integrate-public-pools/
[329] See Cronin, *Direct Democracy,* at 139-141 for a detailed look at the Feinstein recall. Radical left-wing White Panthers, who opposed Feinstein's support of gun-control provisions, started the recall effort. As with the later Gray Davis recall, there was a low ten percent signature requirement to get on the ballot. Other interest groups glommed onto the recall, but Feinstein garnered eighty-one percent of the vote in the election.

Frank Shaw in 1938.[330] Shaw appears to be the last official in Los Angeles to actually be removed. The last of the big city mayors to face a recall was in 2011, when the Omaha Mayor Jim Suttle barely survived a recall and the Miami-Dade Mayor Carlos Alvarez was ousted. Some famous people have fought recall campaigns. Former Congressman and Presidential candidate Dennis Kucinich barely survived a recall when he was mayor of Cleveland in 1978. He is now running for that job again. And filmmaker Michael Moore survived a recall when he was a school board member in Michigan.[331]

After serving as Nebraska's Governor, Charles Bryan faced a recall effort as mayor of Lincoln Nebraska in 1935.[332] Brother of the Great Commoner (William Jennings Bryan), Bryan was the Democratic nominee for Vice President in 1924 (which is the last time the Democrats nominated a Governor for the VP position).[333] In the end it seems that Bryan did not face a recall vote.

Replace Yourself:

On the local level, recalls can be all over the place. In 2018, a Fall River, Massachusetts Mayor Jassiel Correia II lost the recall, but was allowed to run in the replacement race. He won in the five person race. In 1982, Mansfield, Massachusetts Selectman John McNair pulled off this same trick, though three other Selectmen lost their seats in the same election.

Strange Days:

A Moreno Valley School Board Member faced a recall attempt in 2012 after he was charged with attempted murder, rape, pimping and pandering for running a prostitution ring. After the charges were filed, the board member filed to run for City Council. The recall did not get on the ballot as petitioners could not get 9,225 signatures, but the board member did get a prison sentence of 14 years.[334]

Social media and other modern communication follies have played an increasing role in modern recall fights. An Ellicot, Colorado School Board member resigned due to charges that she was sexting with a 14 year old student.[335] A Jefferson Parish President in Louisiana faced a recall for sexting with a 17 year old student, but again they couldn't get the signatures.

Stockton, California Councilman Mark Stebbins faced two recalls in 1984, with the main complaint being that he lied by claiming African-American ethnicity. Stebbins survived the first

---

[330] In addition to Harper, Mayor Frank Shaw was recalled and removed in 1938. Shaw's administration "considered the most corrupt in city's history," was supported by Haynes. Sitton, 243. Haynes died before the Shaw recall.

[331] Michael Moore, "A Recall Election? Been There, Won That at Age 18," *Los Angeles Times*, October 26, 2003. tps://www.latimes.com/archives/la-xpm-2003-oct-03-oe-moore3-story.html

[332] *Fayetteville Daily Democrat*, August 13, 1935. "Bryan Recall Checked," *New York Times*, October 26, 1935.

[333] Joshua Spivak, "The Ultimate Inside-the-Beltway Job," *Washington Post,* March 7, 2004. There have been two her former Governors nominated (Edward Muskie and Joseph Robinson), but they both had since moved to the nate.

[334] Gail Wesson, " Moreno Valley: Assault charges dropped against Mike Rios," *Riverside Press Enterprise,* March 2015. https://www.pe.com/2015/03/06/moreno-valley-assault-charges-dropped-against-mike-rios/ He still had to ve the 14 years (and four months, for you The Wire fans).

[335] She was already facing a recall vote due to a decision to combine schools.

recall in March, but was ousted in December.

Tekonsha Village saw multiple recalls over the appointment of replacements to the council. Trustee Howard Rigg was hit with petitions after he objected to the appointment of the girlfriend of Village President Corey Wood to replace Wood's ex-wife on the council. Rigg then tried to recall Wood. The recall against Wood did not get to the ballot, but the one against Rigg did – and he lost.

In 1913, King's County Superintendent of Schools N.E. Davidson was the first woman kicked out of office in California and perhaps anywhere in the country.[336]

New Jersey has not been a big user of recalls, but the West Wildwood one was worth it. Mayor Herbert Frederick and Commissioner Gerard McNamara survived a 2010 recall. The city later had to pay a $350,000 settlement after they constructed a "retaliation" wall -- a 66 foot long/27-60 inch high wall that was clearly designed to prevent the lead petitioners from using their driveways and garages. I can no longer find the picture online, but hopefully someone else can.[337]

And, as promised in the opening paragraph of the book, in what may be my personal favorite recall, the Charlevoix, Michigan voted out three city councilmembers over a move to put a community fireplace in a park. Why do I like this one? I can't say. It just feels like an old time event, except instead of everyone getting together, they kick some officials out of office.

Comebacks – Is The Recall a Career Ender?

For an elected official, a recall is seen as a career low point. After all, the voters are kicking you out, and not even waiting to the appointed time to do so. But is a recall so bad? Is an ouster by a recall the end of a career? Not always.

At least two officials have managed to lose two recall votes in their career. Fullerton, California Councilman Don Bankhead lost recalls in 1994 and 2012 and Portsmouth, Virginia Mayor James Holley III, lost recalls in 1984 and 2010.While this may look bad, it does show how it is possible to rebound, even if you are then thrown out of office again.

The most obvious example of a great comeback story is the three losers in the North Dakota recalls of 1921. Governor Lynn Frazier was ousted in 1921. In 1922, he was elected to the first of the three US Senate terms. His Attorney General, William Lemke went on to serve five terms in Congress.[338] Agriculture and Labor Commissioner John Hagan got his job back in 1937 and won the Republican nomination for Governor in 1938 (he lost the general election).

---

[336] *"Prescott Daily News*, August 20, 1913.
[337] John Paff, "West Wildwood pays $350,000 to settle retaliation lawsuit filed by local couple," *Transparency NJ* February 22, 2015. Here's the brief filed by the plaintiffs:
https://drive.google.com/file/d/0B66zM58TlOVKZ0Q3Z2YyQnpYTDQ/view?resourcekey=0-C3ooLrW-T_D0qt53qQhJDg
[338] Lemke also ran for President in 1936 on the Union Party ticket. He received over 800,000, putting him 3rd.

Seattle Mayor Hiram Gill lost a recall in 1914 and was back in office the following term. Among our recent recall losers, the 2012 Wisconsin Senate loser Van Wanggaard regained his seat in 2014 and Josh Newman lost his in 2018 and returned to office in 2020.

If losing a recall isn't a career-ender, surviving one can be a rocket boost. Dianne Feinstein beat back the recall in 1983. By 1984 she was being talked about for the VP and was the US Senator by 1992. Jeff Denham survived a recall in 2008, and was then elected to Congress. The same thing happened with recall survivor, Wisconsin Senator Scott Fitzgerald in 2012. James Owens, the second state level official to face recall back in 1914, had previously survived a recall vote as a Los Angeles Councilman.

Scott Walker's recall victory helped propel him to the front ranks of the Republican Party, and made him a legitimate contender for the 2016 presidency.

For Gavin Newsom, this may be a comforting thought for the future.

Conclusion

The Boomerang Effect

As the Gavin Newsom recall election approaches, the one fact that should continue to jump out at us is just how few state-level recalls there have been. With the power of the recall, it seems like it should be a worthwhile gamble. Yet we have seen a number of reasons why this is not so. And there is one more reason worth considering here: The boomerang effect. Even when a recall succeeds it often results in a net loss for the backers who are led to rue the day they started out on what may be a fool's errand. The recall is frequently a weapon of the weak and when it is used, even successfully, it may expose this weakness.

The 1983 recalls in Michigan are one of the few state-level examples that recall backers can look as an unadulterated success. The Republicans have not lost control of the Senate since. But the impact of other recalls has been at best limited, if not straight out detrimental, in the long run. Democrats were not helped by the recalls in Wisconsin in 2011-2012. It took them until the banner Democratic year in 2018 for the party to recapture the Governor's office and (due also to gerrymandering) they are nowhere near to getting back control of either branch of the legislature. Even worse, in 2016 the party lost a presidential race in the state for the first time since 1984. The recall is not to blame, but it certainly didn't help.

Colorado saw two recalls in 2013, and the Democrats had to use a loophole in the law and resign a seat in order to keep control of the Senate. In the next election, they won back those two seats, but they lost control of the Senate. On an issue basis, this recall has not scared Democrats away from supporting gun control.[339] In the larger political realm, the Republicans are on the run in the Rocky Mountain State. The state was so Republican that in 2004, some Democrats proposed splitting its Electoral College vote. Democratic presidential candidates haven't lost the state since. But the recall is still on Republicans' minds. In 2019, the Republicans in the state worked themselves into a fervor to get recalls on the ballot against the governor and various legislators. And what's the result? In 2020, they lost the senate seat and Joe Biden was the first presidential contender to win the state by more than 10% since 1984. Did the recalls – and the recent calls for more recalls – help?

Nevada hasn't seen any recalls, but we've seen repeated threats to use the recall, prior to the 2018 election (see the discussion on voter strike law). The result? The Democrats won the Governor's mansion for the first time this century and Nevada saw the only incumbent Republican senator ousted that year. Did the threats of recalls – some also against Republican leaders by further right groups – help prove to voters that Republicans should be elected?

But California truly tells the tale. By an overwhelming margin, Democrats have been the target of recalls in California. Since 1994, five of the six legislators who have faced a recall have eithe been a Democrat or were targeted because they supported the Democrats. Both Governors were Democrats. The party may feel that the recall is trouble. But this is a short-sighted view.

---

[339] You could make the tenuous argument that it scared Republicans away from any deviation in support, though I haven't seen that suggested anywhere. It is likely that Republicans had long since inculcated this point.

The reason the Democrats faced so many recalls is a positive one for the party. It is because the Democrats have managed to reverse more than a century years of failure in the Golden State and been astonishingly successful over the last three decades.

In 1994, Pete Wilson won re-election as governor, the fourth straight term for Republicans. No surprise there – the Democrats only had control of the governor's mansion for 22 years in the entire 20th Century. In that same election, the Republicans took control of the California Assembly for the first time in 25 years. The Congressional delegation coming out of November was split 26-26. If we take this story back two years, we see that the Republicans held the US Senate seat, which is also no surprise. Before 1992, at least one of the US Senate seats was a held by a Republican for all but six years of the 20th Century. And if we go back a little further, to 1988, we see George H.W. Bush won California's Electoral College vote. No surprise here as well – Bush's victory was the 10th over the last 11 elections. The party could rely on California. In modern parlance, California may have been a purple state, but it was one with a decided red tinge.

Three decades and seven recalls later, we see a new world, one that calls into question any value that Republicans may have received from the recall. Gavin Newsom may be facing a recall, but his 2018 victory was the third straight by a Democrat – the first time the Democrats won three straight gubernatorial elections in California since before the Civil War and the longest stretch of continual Democratic control in the state's history. Since the 2003 recall, the party's registration advantage has gone from less than 9% to over 22%.[340] The Democrats hold veto-proof majorities in both the Senate and Assembly. Democrats have a three-quarters majority in the House Delegation – which is the only reason the Democrats hold the majority and California's Nancy Pelosi holds the Speakership. The US Senate seats are so safely ensconced in Democratic hands that in the last two elections in 2016 and 2018, the Republicans did not have a candidate make the run-off. Nobody thinks the Republicans are going to capture the seat in 2022. And after almost a half century of losses, the Democrats have won California's Electoral College vote for the eighth straight election, winning it by 29 percent. Once again, nobody believes that whoever the Republicans nominate in 2024, they have a chance at capturing California's vote. This means that one-fifth of the margin needed for the presidential victory – larger than the smallest fourteen states combined – can be tattooed into the Democratic column.

Therefore, California is not the Democratic equivalent of Texas or Ohio or Florida. It's not even Mississippi or Kansas. It is far bluer than any of those states are red. California is now the Democrats own Private Idaho.

For Republicans, the recall comes at an odd time. The party actually had a good 2020. Even with the 29% loss, the Republicans managed to capture four house seats. It was the first time since 1994 that they ousted a Democratic incumbent. Instead of building on this success and tilling the soil, the Republicans have looked for the easy fix of recalls. Much as the 2003 recall did not result in any long term benefits to the Republicans, we may see similar problems for the party

---

[340] Some of that could be that Republicans are registering instead as independents or no party preference, but the numbers are stark. Secretary of State's 60-Day Report of Registration on July 16, 2021. tps://www.sos.ca.gov/elections/report-registration/60day-recall-2021

here. Even ousting Newsom is unlikely to result in lasting change in the most valuable state in the country.[341]

Republicans have succeeded in using the recall to oust people. They may succeed again. But the stagnation of the party suggests that they are paying a heavy price for trying the recall shortcut. With those numbers, why is any Democrat discussing changing any political laws whatsoever? If the price of complete domination of the state – a state that was the cause of so much heartache – is that the party has to face a recall every so often, shouldn't they be happy to write that check.

The Technocrats' Dilemma:

Ever since at least John Quincy Adams lost his re-election race, technocrats in America have been on a cold streak. No matter the technical proficiency of any official, in American politics there will be a desire to go with what's exciting behind door number 3. It seems a bit of a surprise that direct democracy did not come out of the Jacksonian Era, but that election effectively decided that running as an expert staring at the sky, rather than someone presenting as a regular person with their ear to the ground, is a bad strategy in America. The recall is not the only, but it is the best example of this rule.

The argument for the recall is based on the benefits of more democracy, including the fact that in most instances, voters specifically approved the recall by a direct vote, frequently overwhelmingly and against opposition from politicians and the power structure. Unlike so much of our political structure, the recall was a stamped with the approval of the population at large. To take the most obvious example, no voter – and possibly no one but judges – voted on the idea that the Supreme Court should have the overarching authority of judicial review. That idea has been accepted by practice. Shouldn't the recall, which was approved by voters, receive at least the same respect?

But let's once again revisit some of the arguments against the recall. That it should only be used for corruption or manifest incompetence is one that voters and the drafters of many recall laws seem to not accept. Cutting a term short under Taft's "Hair-Trigger" complaint for political or policy reasons feels "wrong" in the US, but again, that is more a statement about how the political system operates than a real argument. Electoral structures as a whole have been moving rapidly to a more voter-directed government. This is true, whether it is from direct democracy itself or it is from politicians being vastly more aware of voter opinions on every single issue that crops up

The Trustee argument, that in Hamilton's words, we do not want Senators to be effected by the "capricious humors among the people" is powerful one. But does it hold up? This point for the "trustee" model of government, that we want elected officials to make the big decisions rather

---

[341] This is a topic for another day, but I would argue that the Republicans presidential ascendancy from 1968-1988 was built on the growth of California (note that their two biggest presidential winners were from the state) and the downfall from this control – which has in many ways fueled the party's current extreme anger – is built on losing the state.

an just represent our views,[342] stops short of a more unpleasant and more truthful question. It
es not forthrightly acknowledge the real question -- can the people be trusted to come to a
tter decision than a "trustee"?

the mass of voters are able to have better answers than the single, arguably much more
orthy" trustee, than there should be no problem with a recall. What the argument against the
call is stating is that the mass of voters are more likely to come up with a worse answer. And
hy is that?

eorge Mason University Law Professor Ilya Somin's book Democracy and Political Ignorance
mes up with the honest answer, arguing that voters display shocking political ignorance.[343]
min provides what would be the most valid complaint against direct democracy (though that is
t the goal of the book – he is arguing for "voting with your feet"), namely that trustees have far
tter knowledge and the ability to process the information in order to make the best possible
licy.

espect the argument, though I'm not sure that Somin's correct, at least as it relates to
mething like the recall. Both recent examples, as well as the entirety of recorded human
story, show that we have little reason to believe that politicians would uniformly stand up to a
ore popular and more powerful elected official. In fact, that "gun behind the door" recall may
ve other politicians courage to make a move. Additionally, after reading about thousands of
call attempts, I'm not sure that greater political knowledge means that politicians may have
tter instinct or thought for good decision making than the mass of voters. We have frequently
orified the past as a bi-partisan paradise, but this is simply looking with rose-colored glasses.
ere is no reason to glorify the present, but the inability of earlier generations of leaders to deal
th slavery or Civil Rights suggests that the Trustee model is not some unassailable benefit.

If it wasn't the late breaking quote, I would have opened with this letter, that is probably written as a joke, which
ys on the Trustee/Representative question. "I have received your letter about the Excise and I am surprised at
ur insolence in writing to me at all. You know as I know that I bought this constituency. About what you said
out the excise: may God's curse light upon you and may it make your women as open and as free to the excise
icers as your wives and daughter have always been to me while I have represented your scoundrel corporation
." Anthony Henley, Member of Parliament for Southhampton, circa 1733 Seen on A History Blog:
p://ahistoryblog.com/2013/11/21/anthony-henley-1700-1767-dear-sir-please-go-jump-in-the-lake/
Ilya Somin, Democracy and Political Ignorance: Why Smaller Government is Smarter, Stanford University Press,
3. It also is an example of what attracted many of us to blogs in the first place -- as a universe where you can see
h-level analysis from across the political spectrum. Unfortunately, a lot of that cross-pollination has withered
er the years and has been replaced by partisan rants, but it is still out there. The writings on political ignorance
re the first time I saw someone truly take a detailed, evidence-based attack on what I saw as the underlying
uments in favor of allowing recalls. My goal in studying recalls was not to get rich or famous (mission
omplished!) but to gain a better understanding of a weird, completely ignored corner of the political system, one
I think actually explains a lot about how politics operates in the real world. Only a small part of my writing is on
theoretical and philosophical underpinnings of the recall, but the rest of my writing all grows out from it. The
political analysis should help me hone that understanding, and the exploration of political ignorance has done.

But why the recall?

Like everyone else, you may be asking why I've spent 25 years studying the recall. Does the recall add to our knowledge of the political process? Does it show us something about how America operates?

As you've hopefully seen in the footnotes, I regularly write about many other topics in politics. But the recall provides a window into how politics works at a more granular level. It shows the issues and personal conflicts that truly drive politics and that bubble up to reshape the national agenda. In a strange way, national politics has both gotten more terrifying and vastly more boring. The issues and personalities have been sliced down and the political world has been drained of color. Even more than in the past, politics has become a "my team" event. It's no surprise that working across the aisle has become a rarity. But local politics still has some of the frisson that drew many of us to the subject in the first place.

At the same time, we understand less and less about local issues. The death of local coverage has been a true disaster in America. I suspect that part of the reason for the drop off in reported recalls is that we (Ballotpedia and myself) just don't see them because there is no local newspaper to cover them. As it is, thanks to paywalls, I see much less detail than ever before.

Additionally, the papers that cover stories are focusing only on the national scene. I wrote some of this a few years ago,[344] but I think it hits on one of the big points about the need to look at recalls and other local electoral events. New York Times Public Editor Liz Spayd noted that the paper would be cutting back its coverage of the metro beat, as its editors' looked to focus on stories that have "larger, more consequential themes."[345]

"You can't have your reporters parked in courthouses and police stations all day – or chasing fires – and still deliver memorable, ambitious stories that take time to produce."

That statement has it exactly backward. In fact, you can't really deliver memorable stories if you are not on the ground doing the day-to-day reporting to understand what is happening on the local level. The desire to chase the big exciting scoop or write the long think pieces that win Pulitzer Prizes forces reporters to miss out on the real stories that reveal what is actually happening in the city, country and world. Missing out on the local level stories leads reporters to dismiss many of the major trends that have gripped the country in the last two decades. There is a belief that politics is a top down structure, when in reality it is a bottom-up one. Issues first start boiling up from the local level before they take over the national stage.

On a popular media database, the NYT currently lists 84 names in its Washington, DC bureau. They have one in Albany. From those numbers, you would not realize that state laws frequently have more impact than federal ones. Governor Andrew Cuomo was most of the way through a

---

[344] Joshua Spivak, "All the News that's no longer fit to print: The NYT and the death of local news," *Huffington Post*, September 2, 2016. https://www.huffpost.com/entry/all-the-news-thats-no-longer-fit-to-print-the-nyt_b_57c7d71be4b07addc4114748?fmsbswokx5437hkt9=

[345] Liz Spayd, "A 'New York' Paper Takes a Look in the Mirror," *New York Times*, August 6, 2016.

third term before he was engulfed in scandal over harassment complaints. In recent years, the New York Speaker of the Assembly and the Senate Majority Leader were both convicted of criminal behavior. Despite longtime rumors about both officials, the Times didn't break these stories.

The Times and other papers want memorable groundbreaking stories. They should look and see how stories were broken in the past. In The Powerbroker, Robert Caro points out that one of the big breaks in the fall of Robert Moses started with the basic understanding of neighborhoods that you would get from working a regular beat. It was more garbage cans[346] that helped tip off a reporter to the real scandals of Moses' team.

The recall reveals exactly this. People aggravated over some issue and willing to do something about it – by getting signatures and kicking an elected official out of office. Sometimes it is about "teams" but usually it is a simpler issue than that.

A Slight Discomfort?

If you've gotten this far, or even if you just jumped to the ending, you probably have some views on the wisdom of the recall. You may believe the recall is either critical to American Government or, conversely, a danger to the Republic. I think the evidence shows that neither is true. A look at the last century of use shows that the device has not met the hopes of its creators or the fears of its opponents. It is closer to the "gun behind the door" of Hiram Johnson's estimation than it is Taft's "hair-trigger" firing too quickly. But even the hidden weapon is frequently seen as an empty threat.

Consider the numbers. It's not even clear how many elected positions there are in America -- studies have suggested that there are over 500,000 positions in the US[347] -- nor is it clear how many can face a recall. But what seems certain is that of those nearly half a million positions, somewhere in the neighborhood of 100 (.02%) may face a recall election in any given year, and 300-500 face a recall threat. On the state level, there are 7383 state legislators in the US.[348] In 113 years of the recall on the state level, only 39 have faced a recall election and a third of them were in one session of the Wisconsin legislature.

Because of the personal nature of the recall and the shocking finality of a loss, the recall may be seen by some as on par – and perhaps viewed as more powerful – than the initiative. But this is clearly not the case at all. The initiative is a potential world changing event. The recall's impact

---

[346] Robert Caro, The Powerbroker, Vintage Books, 1975. 963.

[347] Zimmerman, 1. He cites 483,830 local government officers and 18,828 elected state government officers in a 992 Census of Governments. The 2012 Census shows 89,004 local governments, 38,917 general purpose local governments and 50,087 special purpose governments in the US. Also see this post by David Nir in the Daily Kos https://www.dailykos.com/stories/2015/3/29/1372225/-Just-how-many-elected-officials-are-there-in-the-United-States-The-answer-is-mind-blowing citing Jennifer Lawless, Becoming a Candidate, Cambridge University Press, 011.

[348] NCSL Page -- https://www.ncsl.org/research/about-state-legislatures/partisan-composition.aspx though oddly in eir data composition they seem to suggest that there are 7572 legislators – see here. ps://www.ncsl.org/research/about-state-legislatures/legislatures-at-a-glance.aspx. I have no idea why there is a crepancy.

is much more limited.

But the argument that it should be eliminated or heavily constricted runs into the powerful point that the voters want recalls. They have repeatedly voted to adopt recall laws by overwhelming margins, frequently against significant opposition from elected officials and editorial writers. They have used recalls to get the government they want and they have done it without causing too much heartburn to the political process. That seems to be enough of a reason to not mess with the law.

Acknowledgements

Twenty-five years ago, working in a state senate office in Brooklyn, I was looking for a topic for my Master's thesis, when I read two papers on recalls. One footnote particularly caught my attention – that the recall was barely studied. The paper, and my fresh memories of the coverage of the 1995 California recall fight, gave me a path forward.

For the first 15 years, I kept up on the recall, wrote op-eds and an academic paper. It was only in 2011, after a call from the Milwaukee Journal Sentinel's Craig Gilbert, who asked for a full list of state legislatives recall, that I decided that I needed to take a more systematic approach and started the Recall Elections Blog.

I am always asked why the recall. As you hopefully will see, I'm also interested in many other areas of politics. But I will say that at this time politics is not just terrifying but surprisingly boring, drained of color and real personality. There have always been many national politicians who "came to do good, but stayed to do well," but now it seems the goal of a good number of officials is not even personal corruption, but rather using Congress as a way station to get hired as a TV personality.[349] The recall shows a very different political world and puts the spotlight on the still interesting local fights, filled with people so far away from the spotlight that they actually do care about issues.

This book attempts to provide a detailed history of the recall and to explain the many different facets about how the recall operates. Unfortunately, because of the compressed time frame under which I wrote this book, it does not have anywhere near all that I would like to include (nor did it have the professional editors to polish it), but I hope that the reader receives a fuller understanding of the recall while voting is still going on. In the future, I hope to present a systematic approach to local recalls. Despite the warnings of others, I have chosen to use footnotes (in the e-book, they were transformed into endnotes) so you can see both the sources in real time and my other thoughts on subjects that I thought would slow down the text. I didn't really follow any style in the footnotes, except to make the source document itself accessible, if possible.

The book had quite a bit more humor in the earlier iterations, as well as many different music lyrics, but due to the vagaries of copyright law, I alas had to take them out. Maybe you'll see them on the blog. There's some recall trivia[350] here, but nowhere near enough for my taste. I choose a very basic title so it is easy to find and understand, though, in a nod to the early history, I really did want to consider something using "Gun behind the Door" or "Hair-Trigger" or perhaps "The High Bouncing Lover of Recalls." Oh well.

---

[49] One tip here – if you know the name of a very junior member of the House, chances are they're probably not good at the "serving in Congress" function, but only good at the "racing to the camera to say something outrageous" ortion of the job. Thanks to social media, the showhorse vs. workhorse divide has never been this stark or one-ided.

[0] I did want to include Baseball trivia (the best trivia question answer is always Babe Ruth, but as a pitcher) but gain, alas. However, I will put in one question right here which I'll answer on the blog on September 14: "Who is e first player to play (and win) two World Series rings (pretending that they had rings back then)?"

I'd like to thank a number of people who were instrumental in bringing this book to fruition and I apologize to anyone I leave off. I guess I can start with Yonatan Jacobs, who ordered the original article that set me off on this odd journey, when we both worked for Senator Seymour Lachman. Senator Lachman not only hired me for that job, but brought me aboard when he founded the Hugh L. Carey Institute for Government Reform at Wagner College, which I have been fortunate enough to be affiliated with for more than a decade.

My late Professors Hans L. Trefousse, my thesis advisor, and Ari Hoogenboom helped lay the groundwork for my historical knowledge. Dr. Paul Thomsen gave me advice on this book, as well as the idea to use a mask on the cover.

Allan Ripp and the entire team of Ripp Media has been a fantastic place to work for almost two decades now and his support and enthusiasm for my extra-curricular writing has been nothing short of inspiring. My friend and long-time colleague Keith Emmer has been a great help in discussing this book and by sending back important edits that greatly improved the grammar and readability of the text.

I have been fortunate to deal with an enormous number of journalists and editors over the years, spanning the entire partisan divide and almost without exception I've found them to be knowledgeable, open-minded and relentlessly curious to understand how and why a political process works. I cannot cite all the reporters, but we should be happy that they are on the ramparts of democracy, doing their best to keep the system honest.

I do want to cite some of the bloggers who have been particularly helpful in the early going. Election Law Blogger Rick Hasen was, in many ways, the inspiration for the Recall Election Blog and has been a longtime source of support. Ten years ago, Daily Kos' David Nir wrote me that when he first saw the blog, he expected it to be another fly-by-nighter, which would last three months or so. Fortunately, he has been a source of encouragement and someone who has asked important questions that expanded the knowledge of how recalls work in practice. I've also received early encouragement from the Volokh Conspiracy and the Political Wire's Taegan Goddard. In the early days, that recognition was important for anyone running the solitary endeavor of a blog.

While much of the recent work has been online, this is not true about my earlier research, and I'd like to thank the libraries of Brooklyn College, the Library of Congress, Columbia Law School and the Doe Library of UC Berkeley and I thank them for their help.

I'd like to thank my parents who helped read and edit this book (as well as my thesis many years ago) among many other helpful actions (including arguably "funding" the early research)[in the course of understanding the recall], as well as my grandparents, who I've written about in the past and one of whom will at least get to read this book. While I'm the only one of my siblings interested in politics, somehow all three of them seem to get a kick out of the fact that I have this seemingly weird knowledge. I can't say my two children, Charlie and Ezra, are recall super-fans, but they may be the only people who will end up being forced to read this book.

all these years of work, there has been only one person who did not think studying recall
ections was a sign of clear insanity. In fact, she's probably the only person who thought
rting a blog and writing papers on this subject was a great use of time. Not only that, she was
e only person who read this document more than once and her critical corrections undoubtedly
proved it immensely, which is just part of the reason why I dedicated this book to my wife.

Made in the USA
Las Vegas, NV
13 October 2021